SPECTRE of the STRANGER

D1342395

"A lucid post-metaphysical meditation. Bazzano skilfully weaves together disparate strands of thought from Europe and Asia, which converge in an unconditional embrace of the secular, the immediate and, above all, the other."

Stephen Batchelor, author of *Confession of a Buddhist Atheist*

"This book is challenging, witty, and erudite. The range of topics and authors is both admirable and enviable as is the writer's facility in weaving together unexpected associations that provoke new mental reverberations. I greatly admire the book."

Prof. Ernesto Spinelli, author of *Practising Existential Psychotherapy*

"In this provocative and learned book, Manu Bazzano shows himself to be a bold adventurer of ideas. Bringing together the central insight of Buddhism, the insubstantial nature of the self, and the exploration of 'otherness' which has preoccupied European philosophy over the last century, the author offers an exciting exploration through a rich banquet of ideas drawn from Western philosophy, classical mythology, psychotherapy theory and Zen Buddhism. At once erudite and very readable, his poetic style carries the reader through landscapes of thought which are both colourful and thought provoking. His message is visionary, but yet advocates an approach grounded in the detailed fabric of ordinariness. His writing embodies the paradoxes which he explores, inviting true encounter with the other and the stranger as the route to the personal, the social, the spiritual and the ethical."

Caroline Brazier, author of *Buddhist Psychology*

SHREWSBURY COLLEGE LIBRARY

Inv No. Date 12/9/13
202-1296473
Ord No. 968 0355 Date

Class No. BAZ

Price £11.16   Checked T

"Manu Bazzano takes us on a fascinating journey through philosophy, religion, psychotherapy, and politics which challenges us to recognise – and welcome – the stranger, both in others and in ourselves. This beautifully written and poetic book exemplifies the very relationship that is called for, and confronts us directly with many of the comforting strategies we use to avoid encountering otherness. This is a timely call to a radical ethics which could transform the ways in which we relate: from the interpersonal realms of the romantic relationship or the therapeutic encounter, to the global arenas of war and migration."

Dr Meg Barker, Senior Lecturer in Psychology, Open University

"Manu Bazzano invites you to leave the home of habitual understanding (including the ivory tower of mainstream philosophy) and enjoy the wide, open landscape. En route you will meet Ulysses and Abraham; at times you'll walk with Lévinas and Nietzsche, Agamben, Lefebvre and Merleau-Ponty. At the end of your journey you will notice that you are back at home meeting yourselfboth as a stranger and as an intimate friend. You will also notice that you have found yourself – by unfolding the hospitality of your own Buddha-nature."

Jürgen Kriz, Professor of Psychotherapy and Clinical Psychology,
University of Osnabrück

"I found this book a delight and a constructive irritation. Suggesting a path beyond alienation that debunks our social pretensions, it is full of sparkling original and provocative ideas which come at one in a torrent. You will find a multiplicity of new angles and glittering images, illuminating what might otherwise remain abstruse, and cross fertilizing what one might never have brought together. I found many charming turns of phrase that said things I have been trying to say for years and some, equally well phrased, that challenged my foundations. This is a book that seeks to provoke solipsism and to challenge us to go beyond the will, inprisoned by the ego as it is, into the free fall of that space that is the nurturer of our dreams and in which we are, all at once, both host and exile."

David Brazier, author of *Zen Therapy*

SPECTRE of the STRANGER

Towards a Phenomenology of Hospitality

MANU BAZZANO

sussex
ACADEMIC
PRESS
Brighton • Portland • Toronto

Copyright © Manu Bazzano, 2012.

The right of Manu Bazzano to be identified as Author of this work has been asserted in accordance with the Copyright, Designs and Patents Act 1988.

2 4 6 8 10 9 7 5 3 1
2

First published in 2012 by
SUSSEX ACADEMIC PRESS
PO Box 139
Eastbourne BN24 9BP

and in the United States of America by
SUSSEX ACADEMIC PRESS
920 NE 58th Ave   Suite 300
Portland, Oregon 97213-3786

and in Canada by
SUSSEX ACADEMIC PRESS (CANADA)
8000 Bathurst Street, Unit 1, PO Box 30010, Vaughan, Ontario L4J 0C6

All rights reserved. Except for the quotation of short passages for the purposes of criticism and review, no part of this publication may be reproduced, stored in a retrieval system or transmitted in any form or by any means, electronic, mechanical, photocopying, recording or otherwise, without the prior permission of the publisher.

British Library Cataloguing in Publication Data
A CIP catalogue record for this book is available from the British Library.

Library of Congress Cataloging-in-Publication Data
Bazzano, Manu.
Spectre of the stranger : towards a phenomenology of hospitality / Manu
  Bazzano.
  p. cm.
Includes bibliographical references (p.   ) and index.
ISBN 978-1-84519-538-0 (p/b : alk. paper)
  1. Hospitality. 2. Self. 3. Other (Philosophy) 4. Phenomenology.
5. Zen Buddhism. I. Title.
BJ2021.B39 2012
177'.1—dc23

                                                            2012016047

Typeset and designed by Sussex Academic Press, Brighton & Eastbourne.
Printed by TJ International, Padstow, Cornwall.
This book is printed on acid-free paper.

CONTENTS

CONTENTS

Contents

ACKNOWLEDGMENTS

I like to thank those who directly or indirectly helped me give shape to this book: Nigel Armistead for his painstaking editing work and invaluable suggestions, Alex Gooch and Darius Cuplinskas for their insights, Ernesto Spinelli for his detailed comments, Stephen Batchelor for inspiration, and Sarita Doveton for her ongoing support and for enduring my philosophical musings with great patience.

This book is dedicated to the memory of
my grandfather, Santo Bazzano,
who emigrated from his native Calabria to New York
in the first years of the twentieth century

Who loves the stranger?
Who else is there to love?
(Jacques Derrida)

. . . justice, not metaphysics.
(Geoffrey Hill)

A spectre is haunting Europe . . .
(Marx & Engels)

INTRODUCTION

I started writing this book as a rebellion against the absolute – only to realize, half way through, that there is no such thing. Most philosophical and religious traditions speak of two worlds, even though the language they use differs. Zen Buddhism speaks of the *absolute* and the *relative* dimensions: "like two arrows, meeting in mid air", they are said to fit one another "as a box and its lid". Or so goes the recitation of the sutras. In reality, there seems to be a preference for the absolute, for 'enlightenment', often understood as a breakthrough to a 'God's-eye view'. We find the same division in Hellenism: instead of absolute and relative, the Greeks used the terms *being* and *becoming*. Hegel similarly wrote of *infinite* and *finite*, and in Hinduism we find a distinction between *Brahman* and *Maya*. In art and in literature, as in our habitual language, we distinguish between the sublime and the ordinary.

And yet, alongside this mainstream philosophical view, a different perspective has developed which focuses on the appreciation of the givens, or gifts, of the everyday and on its unfathomable nature – a perspective which refrains from metaphysical pretensions. Another positive result of this stance is a democratization of the entire spiritual and philosophical endeavour. Over the years, I have noticed and grown wary of the tendency, prevalent among explorers of the human potential, which emphasizes transcendence and enlightenment to the detriment of the everyday dimension into which we are thrown. This is often accompanied by the cult of personality directed at teachers, therapists and facilitators and kept alive by the pervasive belief that these people have crossed a threshold earning them permanent access to a dimension denied to mortals. This tendency is at odds with the cultivation of doubt and perplexity, essential attributes in any enquiry wishing to travel a little further than the metaphysical shopping mall. It is also at variance with the emphasis, in Zen Buddhism as well as in humanistic psychology, on everyday reality. Zen reminds us that ordinary mind is the Buddha; Carl Rogers reminds us that the actualizing tendency is "always up to something".

The yearning for the absolute is nevertheless enticing and I do feel a kinship with the aspirations and the claims of the Romantics, with the flight of Icarus and the feverish visions of Rimbaud. If, on the one hand, they warn us against the dangers of a life consummated by too great a thirst for the sublime, the biographies of Kierkegaard, Genet, Van Gogh, Jimi Hendrix, and Sylvia Plath continue to ignite the imagination. Whereas artists transmute their yearning into a perilous dedication to the Muses, spirituality and psychology devotees invariably convey this longing in the language of *totality*: the day after their conversion or revelation, they become confident purveyors of truth and (invariably second-hand) metaphysics.

Idealists of every creed hurriedly dismiss the everyday because they see it as dualistic. In deciding to pay attention to it, I ran into the difficult domain of ethics and morality. Throughout the book I emphasize the difference between *morality* and *ethics*: I see morality as the set of introjected norms of civil life, the conscience that is nearly always bad conscience, whereas I understand ethics as the attempt to respond adequately to the other. Morality turns a person into a bourgeois. Ethics turns a person into a citizen. Morality produces interiority-as-repentance. Ethics introduces exteriority as reality.

Twentieth century ethics inherited the mighty deconstruction of morals carried out by Nietzsche. It took several decades and the unfolding of an ambiguous cultural movement, phenomenology, to accelerate the dismantling of morality and metaphysics, a process which contributed to the advent of our post-metaphysical era.

It may seem odd to speak of a post-metaphysical era now that religious wars are back in fashion, but the virulent revival of dogmatism we are witnessing at present is born out of the decline of metaphysical certainties.

Levinas was the first to introduce a startling element in philosophy: he located the foundation of ethics not in religion or universal

2

reason, but in phenomena themselves and particularly in the *face* of the other. He did not reach this position at random but after having patiently dismantled the philosophy of Heidegger, a thinker he himself had introduced to the French-speaking world.

Reading Levinas is a remarkable experience: a sincere confrontation with his thought demands nothing less than a careful dismantling of the entire edifice of identity on which traditional western thought is built, an undoing which has repercussions in philosophy, psychology and politics. When I first started writing this book, I tried to articulate the impact this mode of thought had on me; four years later, with the book completed, I can say, not without a sense of relief, that I am free of Levinas. Some may recognize how an original thought becomes sooner or later a new constraint; others may be familiar with the insidious anxiety of influence which makes us worry to be growing under the foliage of a mighty tree that restores yet limits us.

Levinas's position too easily lends itself to the injunctions of the super-ego, and the response to the other slips into a post-modern version of the old patriarchal order. Unlike Buber, Levinas, a Talmudic scholar before being a phenomenologist, sadly failed to recognize otherness in the face of the Palestinians. I believe that Levinas's phenomenology gives us nevertheless the foundation for constructing a *radical ethics* through a widening of the personal and relational spheres into the social and political dimensions, in search of subjects who can represent otherness in the era of globalized capitalism.

I had not anticipated that by investigating contemporary ethics I would stumble into the minefield of politics. I knew that researching and writing a book can take one to unexpected places: *Buddha is dead* had begun with the relatively simple intention of paying tribute to Nietzsche and the Zen tradition, but in the process I encountered psychotherapy, first as a client and then, as the cliché of the wounded healer dictates, by becoming a fully-fledged practitioner.

The current book too had surprises in store: I found themes which I had abandoned in 1980, the year I left for India, at the peak of a turbulent experience with the students' movement and the Italian radical Left. I cannot claim that many will identify with this path, but some readers may find reverberations and even a sort of indirect encouragement.

We used to say the personal is political, and I think this still holds true. But all too often care of self becomes solipsism, while political activism becomes projection onto an external enemy. Both in *Discipline and Punish* and *History of Sexuality*, Foucault expressed two theses which disoriented the orthodox Marxists of the time. The first one maintains that in modern society power has no definite locus but is de-centred (which makes the siege of the Winter Palace redundant). The second is an even more provocative statement: there is no external power but we ourselves are integral to it – which makes it nearly impossible to conceive a clash with the power *out there*. Rather than constituting an impasse, these two theses invite us to study subjectivity directly and initiate a process of dis-identification with the central axioms of coercive power.

In carrying on his research, Foucault focused, during his last lectures at the *Collège de France* in the nineteen eighties, on Hellenism and care of self. Some erroneously interpreted this as a return to traditional subjectivity, but studying and observing the self does not imply *substantiating* the self. One could argue that Buddhist meditation is precisely this: phenomenological investigation, patient dismantling of a fictitious entity, a process which is at variance with the Judaeo-Christian vision and mainstream western philosophy which both understand interiority as repentance. Perhaps it would not have been necessary for westerners to resort to the Buddha's teachings if western culture had paid attention to investigations alive but marginal in the very heart of European culture. In Montaigne, for instance, introspection leads to discovery of the fluid and contradictory nature of the self rather than to the operatic parables of repentance and redemption. To study the self is a form of observation akin to Montaigne's sceptical and ironic procedures of investigation and to the exploratory methods taught by the Buddha. Self-inquiry elicits the dismantling of traditional philosophical categories and of the very notion of power. One needs to experience the insubstantiality of the self in order to understand the insubstantiality of the expanded self, i.e. the nation-state, as well as the insubstantiality of the cosmic self (God, transcendental consciousness, *atman* and so forth).

4

In **Part I**, I discuss the notions of identity and otherness. Identity is conventionally constructed *against* otherness. My place in the sun implies your place in the cold. The identity that emerges out of this conventional perspective is not the singularity that emerges out of mutual recognition but individualism, an isolated a solipsistic view of the self. What I aim to show is that a different kind of interdependent relation exists between identity and otherness, out of which individuality born. The name for this interdependent relation is *hospitality*. Throughout **Part I** I move back and forth between two hypotheses, one inspired by the Zen Buddhist tradition, the other motivated by the philosophy of otherness as expounded by some influential thinkers in the last few decades. The first maintains that there is no such thing as interiority; it asserts the non-substantiality and ineffability of the self. When we look closely, we do not find a thing we can call the self, distinct from phenomena. Consciousness itself emerges from phenomena. The idea I have of myself is another phenomenon just as the traffic noise, the birdsong in this late summer morning. I simply cannot know myself as a solid and separate entity. The *I* too belongs to exteriority. I am external to myself, unknowable to myself; a *stranger* to myself. The *I* itself belongs to otherness. *Je est un autre*: I is another, Rimbaud's famous phrase is, as we shall see, open to several meanings. Identity begins to falter as observation becomes more precise.

The second hypothesis is that only through hospitality true identity is born. Summoned by another, called to respond, the response *creates* me. Called to respond, I step into that shared domain that the neurologist and philosopher Kurt Goldstein,[1] forerunner of Gestalt psychology and a man inspired by Goethe, calls *the immediate*. Called to respond, to be a host to the other, I recognize that an autarchic existence is sheer illusion. It is easy to mistake the domain of the immediate with the inter-subjective and dialogical domains. The latter – now canonical in contemporary psychology – emphasizes the relational aspect of the encounter between two or more subjectivities and confirms the notion of identity rather than questioning it. It also misconstrues the notion of interdependence, common to Buddhism

5

and existential phenomenology. *Inter-subjectivity* is the way in which mainstream western philosophy – steeped as it is in Judaeo-Christian values – translates (and in doing so largely betrays) groundlessness, by safely inscribing it in the Christian notion of love of one's neighbour. Laudable as it might be, such notion averts our gaze from the terror which arises when stumbling upon the insubstantiality of the self.

A perspective rooted in otherness also overturns the Platonic idea of maieutics and the very meaning of experience. The process of education is then no longer seen as extracting pre-existent knowledge and wisdom but instead as the product of an encounter with otherness.

Striving to translate the previous statements into the social and political domains, in **Part II** I go in search of myths and cultural matrixes which justified hostility towards otherness. Relying on Regina Schwartz's seminal study on the Bible,[2] I have traced the origin of nationalism and xenophobia in monotheism, or rather *monolatry*, i.e. the superstitious belief in an exclusive and exclusivist deity. Hospitality, or even *xenophilia* (love of strangers), is then the opposite stance, no less than a revolution, albeit a *human revolution* (the title of **Part II** which is also an expression used by Marx in the 1840s) – a political, but also ethical and aesthetic revolution.

By opening the borders to capital and to the profit of the elites, globalization has exacerbated the condition of millions who have become refugees, migrants, non-citizens and effectively *non-persons*. If individuality comes to light through openness to the other, in the wider social sphere the citizen becomes a citizen by opening up to the experience of the non-citizen. Only thus he becomes a true citizen, for it is only a full recognition of vulnerability which defines human goodness and the meaning of justice itself.[3]

In an attempt to redefine an emancipative praxis, migrants may come to embody (alongside those who live at the margins of globalization's air-conditioned nightmare) a new revolutionary subjectivity after the disappearance of the proletariat. The ethical response marries political activism and renews the tradition of anarchism, substituting the classic notion of individual emancipation of the anarchist tradition with responsibility towards otherness and revolutionary violence with a combative pacifism, civil disobedience and direct action.

In **Part III** I have attempted to delineate the connection between the ethical and the aesthetic dimension. By introducing a symbolic dimension one might avoid the danger of a too-literal interpretation of injunctions and obligations which can be easily hijacked by moral impositions. *Poetry*, understood in a wider sense, is the term I propose in the attempt to avoid the subjugation to the totalizing imperatives of religion and science. It indicates, rather than defines, otherness in the area of identity, of relating, and in the political domain.

Inspired by Hölderlin's statement *dwelling poetically on this Earth*, it reasserts hospitality first and foremost as the poetic act of a subject who never forgets his or her status as a passenger and a guest on this Earth.

PART

I

A PLACE IN THE SUN

Gone with the Wind

At the dawn of western culture we find two cities, Athens and Jerusalem, and two figures, Ulysses and Abraham. Ulysses represents the candour and arrogance of science. Fastidiously Hegelian, he is the sailor whose wanderings never distract him from the goal of returning to Ithaca and to *ipseity*. No matter how disquieting or enlightening, how monstrous or wonderful, experiences are duly assimilated by a subject whose sturdiness and capacity for dialectical synthesis is rarely dented.

To Abraham, a central figure in Judaism, we owe not so much the ambivalent legacy of monotheism, with its obligation of violent devotion to an exclusivist deity, but rather the positive affirmation of exodus.

From Athens we have accepted the official story elaborated by Socrates, Plato, and Aristotle. We accept it complacently, for all in all it satisfies a need for consistency between idealism and rationality. At the same time we admire from a distance, and not without some trepidation, the sacrificial fury and Dionysian rowdiness stemming from Sophocles and Euripides while forgetting, or interpreting one-sidedly, figures considered to be marginal such as Epicurus and Heraclitus.

As for Jerusalem, we take for granted that its contribution consists in the one-God perspective and forget the centrality of exile, that is, the vision of humans as transient, and the refusal to give in to an atavistic attachment to the soil.

For two centuries Europe has undergone a process of de-provincialization, opening itself up to eastern cultures. Ambivalent from

9

the start, this process was inaugurated by Schopenhauer's interest in Buddhism, an interest tainted by influential misreadings that continue to this day and play a role in seeing Buddhism as a life denigrating worldview.

Central to the Buddha's teachings is neither pessimism nor the passivity of contemplation, but the *desertion of one's place in the sun*, the relinquishment of one's illusory roots in ipseity. This is an act of rebellion: it is no less than the *refusal to be* and as such upturns the very basis on which, from Plato through Heidegger, mainstream philosophy rests. It is effectively an act of robbery in the headquarters of ontology. Understanding these teachings implies an individual conversion as well as a shift in the archetypal structures of Hellenic and Judaeo-Christian cultures: Ulysses does not return to Ithaca; Abraham remains loyal to a primary complicity with the wind.

Incitement to Desertion

One of the most significant experiences in my years of Zen practice has been participating in a street retreat. Together with a dozen other practitioners, I lived for three days the life of a homeless person in the streets of London. It was an attempt to open up to their experience and try to understand that "they" are not different from "us". Criticized by many, perhaps rightly, as patronizing and condescending towards the less fortunate, the experience has nevertheless helped me to feel empathy towards the homeless. The implications are not only social, but linked to a practice which is central in Zen Buddhism: relinquishment of self, an act of desertion of status and prestige. Trying to embrace voluntarily a condition from which others try to escape is an act of surrender, and it challenges what in effect is a taboo: to momentarily abandon the certainty of the self undermines everything upon which rests the solidity of civil society.

Deserting one's place in the sun is not otherworldly renunciation but ethical and social action prompted by the knowledge that *my place in the sun means your place in the cold*. It oversteps the atavism of identity through voluntary self-disorientation and displacement, an act suitable for a poet or, some might say, for an idiot.

The self comes to light by venturing into the non-self, by moving inside multiplicity and coming into contact with groundlessness. By deconstructing the self we gain access to a disquieting and exhilarating fluidity; *we enter the stream*, an image shared by both the Buddha and Heraclitus. Entering the stream and accepting the polyvalent, contradictory nature of the self does not imply a disintegration of identity. Some believe that upholding a sort of *monotheism* of the psyche, by sustaining the archetype of self (parallel to the archetype of God) is essential to mental health.[1] I believe the reverse is true. Entering the stream is accepting the challenge of being human without clutching on to a notion of totality; it is allowing plurality (*polytheism* of the psyche) through a process of actualization. Democracy in the psyche is as desirable as democracy in the *polis*. Acceptance of, and dialogue with various deities creates greater fluidity without the regulatory intervention of a 'Self', echo and reverberation of the God of monolatry.

Individuation is Loss

Any civilization worth the name harbours the longing for the impossible, a desire of emancipation from the limitations of the real, the belief that utopia is individually and politically realizable. Only a poet – or an idiot – would dare attempt, or even *become* the change. And only a poet would dare to introduce changes in the language, hence in the perception of the real.

To relinquish ipseity and let go of one's place in the sun is an act of revolt undermining being at its foundations. From Rousseau to Wilde and Thoreau, philosophical rebellions of the past ended up strengthening, in spite of their iconoclastic fervour and beauty, the bourgeois idea of a self-sufficient 'I', a notion reproduced *ad infinitum* by the capitalist enterprise, the work ethics, and the cult of adventurous discovery into unexplored (soon to be colonized) territories of the non-self.

Relinquishing the ego's daydreams of conquest and renouncing self-interest does not imply passivity: when it is no longer the anxiety of appropriation that prompts a motion towards exteriority, *desire* will come along to replace it. This might not bring about real satisfac-

11

tion, yet desire thrusts us into the arms of the other; it sets us up for the inevitable fall from which we will emerge transformed.

In objectless desire, the excursion beyond the borders of ipseity has value because we are exposed to the reverberation of otherness. In a similar way, *individuation* itself is rupture and loss, and exile is the adventure bringing the exiled closer to the truth of life's groundlessness. Weizmann, theoretician of political Zionism, conceived instead exile as an abnormal state from which one can be cured by being integrated into the bosom of a nation or indeed by the creation of a new homeland. In the hazardous psychic landscape of exile, both the dangers of messianic and nationalist dogma come to hatch (cultivated by the spirit of revenge which takes possession of the dispossessed psyche), but also perhaps a breakthrough to a more authentic dimension.

Desire, Shame, and Guilt

Search for pleasure, chastised by moralists of all churches, makes us lean beyond the boundary of being and exposes us to the other. By leaning out of my dwelling, I instigate, whether I want it or not, the twice-risky process of affectivity: by externalizing desire, by acting, I deliberately limit the range of possibilities once limitless in contemplation; I also open myself up to the wounds of embarrassment (the shame of exposed nudity) and disappointment.

In bourgeois morality, as in the bourgeois ethics of work and profit, the risk is instead minimal. Conjugal love can at times slip into the routine of a habitual dimension in which which we pretend to know the unknowable and in so doing empty out the sheer mystery of life. Entrepreneurial capitalist adventure is based on gain and evaluates loss as momentary *debacle* to learn from in view of future gain. The bourgeois cannot admit to internal divisions, to the cracks and inconsistencies in his psyche, because these would threaten the illusory solidity of ipseity, i.e. the superstitious belief in the self as an entity identical to itself. "The bourgeois – Pasolini reminds us – has always [. . .] possessed; the thought of not possessing never occurred to him".[2]

Need and desire open our primary wound. Inauthenticity makes us human, opening us to the sumptuous gifts of revealed nudity. In the motion towards exteriority, I open myself to the fullness of being, no longer *being* as conceived by traditional thought – ipseity, power, independence – but instead *otherness*. I lean out through desire. Desire steers me dangerously towards the other. Once my nakedness (vulnerability, finitude, imperfection) is exposed, shame arises, i.e. the inability to make others forget my essential nudity.

It is in the mutual disclosure of the wound that communication can take place. For the Heidegger of *Parmenides*, shame is a mood or an "emotional tonality" suffusing being; it is an ontological feeling, the very shame of being. Levinas, on the other hand, directly defines shame as the radical impossibility to escape ourselves in order to hide ourselves from ourselves.

In the crisis following disappointment and shame, the possibility of conversion emerges, not as a transcendental occurrence but as vertigo, nausea and malaise revealing our finitude (having, inhabiting, *being a body*). Normally we shun vertigo, searching instead for maps and beaten tracks, paying tribute to the conventional modes of escape and the stale rituals of transcendence. Yet there is also a possibility of escape within the very roots of our mortal coil: there is transcendence *within* immanence, eternity as the quickening existence of a single ephemeral being, as poetic daring which brings us to the meeting of sea and sky on the horizon.

Guilt has a place in the project of revaluation of ethics proposed in these pages, especially if set in opposition to the narcissistic notion of "self-actualization". In small doses, and free from the pathology of religious injunctions, guilt may mitigate the arrogance of an ego (individual as well as collective) who has lost any sense of measure. A genuine feeling of regret could indeed be good medicine for those contemporary political leaders who brazenly escaped sentences destined for war criminals.

At the same time there exists an ideology of guilt, particularly the guilt of the survivor, supported by the assumption that the survivor is innocent yet somehow *obliged to feel guilty*. This assumption is questionable because it urges pandering to a guilt instigated by the super-ego's more punitive configuration. It is questionable also because it presents a generic and "diplomatic" response to problems which are severe precisely in their specificity. Admission of collective guilt here becomes a way to duck the inability to cope with an ethical problem. Germans readily declared their collective guilt after the defeat of Nazism but there was little readiness to identify individuals responsible for the atrocities. The Catholic Church similarly recognized, via the French episcopate, their collective guilt with regards to the Jews but never admitted the serious complicity of Pope Pius XII with Fascism and Nazism.

The unprecedented level of cruelty unleashed during the twentieth century prompts us to reconsider traditional ethical categories and to ask, with Agamben, whether it is still relevant to use as a model the tragic paradigm of the classic and the idealist era, or whether we should choose instead the Nietzschean overcoming of resentment – or if it were indeed better, in view of the magnitude of the massacres committed, to resort to resentment pure and simple. But horror cannot be erased: it eternally recurs in the victims' psyche, in their dreams and memories. And yet a radical ethics based of solidarity and conscious response to otherness cannot withdraw an active affirmation of existence.

Two Common Idolatries

If we go beyond the compulsion to ontology, both spirituality and paganism prove to be idolatrous practices and foundational ideologies.

Spirituality seeks a foundation in transcendental notions, hoping to find nourishment in the barren nipples of tradition. It ferries souls to the other shore and neglects the gifts of *this* shore, incommensurable in the face of finitude. In its paradoxical trajectory, spirituality ends up reinforcing ipseity, and this non-journey of solidification of the self is soundtracked by reassuring homilies and consolatory mantras. In fact, spirituality still keeps us bound to the self and the world whilst regaling us with the exalted fantasy that we are pursuing an elevated path.

Paganism (the second idolatry, the second obstacle to the full appreciation of becoming) is worship of the roots, failure to imagine any disentanglement from the to and fro of the world, from the swampy soil and the tentacles of the flesh, from the vortex of passions and the protective spider web woven around identity and possessions. Paganism demands a wall around one's own fragile idea of the world, around the terror we feel when faced with the inexorability of time and the unpredictability of events.

The necessary rebellion against the ontologism inherent in both spirituality and paganism is individual, yet *individual* here means something different from Cartesian solipsism. We owe much to Descartes, especially the notion of *separation*, which generates, in the third Cartesian meditation on the relation between the *res cogitans* and the infinity of God, *thought beyond thought*, thought as inextinguishable longing. Yet rebellion is here the rebellion of an *individualized* being; orphaned and exiled from his tribe, whose morals and religious dictates she dares dispute in the name of a painful and exhilarating search for authenticity. An individual thus understood constructs an ethical response on the ashes of coercive norms, categorical imperatives and universalizing truths. Radical ethics emerges from the twilight of duty: it is an aporetic, that is to say a paradoxical response. To those who fear that this would unleash moral relativism, one could say that it is important, in spite of the risk, to defend the inalienable freedom and responsibility of the individual as the only effective locus of transformation and independence.

Desire and Longing

Desire is movement towards exteriority. Its trajectory is regally useless; not only of no use, but also outside the project of Eros, who is after union. Unlike Eros, desire is longing for the impossible. Because of desire, the self leaves its dwelling and leaps through the vicissitudes of the loss of self and into the domain of experience. Yet when desire gives in to the mirage of Eros, it congeals into the *project*: poetry becomes prose, dance becomes catwalk, and *Mitsein* (being-with) becomes *Mitmarschieren* (marching-with).

The Devil is Dead

The world has not only lost God but also the Devil; since then, demonization of the other has become as crucial as hagiolatry. The ruinous and sovereign flight from identity is also flight from the particular tribal group we once belonged to. In deserting the group, I also evade what more or less consciously I perceive to be the neurosis intrinsic to the group. For Freud, a group is a micro-climate creating its own universe and its own vision of the world; a group is mad by definition, self-enclosed and self-absorbed. This of course may apply not only to eccentric *new age* congregations and fundamentalist cells, but to any group, including much larger ones such as institutionalized religions and nation-states.

Ethics of the Caress

Is it possible to formulate an ethics of the caress following the contours of the body – not grasping or possessing, but stalking instead the ungraspable future? Such ethics would dare the impossible: to solve (dissolve) the atavism of hatred – inevitable as love – and with a Promethean gesture become free of the God of Cain and Abel, from the partisan God of discord who approves the sacrifice offered by one but rejects the other's. One needs to dare devotion to the other without swearing fidelity to the possessive God of Abraham – to dare define by 'otherness' the entire existence, including the self.

In the attempt to elaborate a radical ethics it is difficult not to repeat the 'Anglo-Saxon' mistake Nietzsche attributed to George Eliot, i.e., getting rid of God and liturgy yet subscribing to Christian morality.

Otherness has to be recognized first of all as exteriority. In his play *The Persians*, Aeschylus teaches us imaginative empathy, which focuses on the suffering of the defeated rather than the jubilation of the winners. He invites Athenians citizens, after the victory at Salamis against the Persians, to think in a radical way, to cultivate a thought external to their experience and to consider the Persians's grief.

Forgiving the Unforgivable

Authentic forgiveness has no motivation. We forgive the unforgivable, since only the unforgivable can be forgiven. Forgiveness is a gratuitous act. Through each successful attempt at forgiving, we create a new horizon. Through forgiveness the past is erased, chains one had imagined indestructible are broken, the *karma* one had believe insurmountable is left behind. Karma itself is revealed as a religious postulate. Forgiveness dissolves identity, revealed as the unsustainable and vain edifice on whose foundation even the healthy radicalism of the second part of the twentieth century has dwelled – with its emphasis on the search for roots, discovery of ancestors, exploration of the soil and the entire spectrum of the myths of belonging; with its emphasis on historic memory, aimed at the reification of one's artificial notion of identity. How much more stimulating is the art of forgetting! Forgetting and forgiving are twin acts. The rancorous remembers everything. The pathology of rancour and revenge engenders our idolatrous craving for power. Power itself is pathology, and so is craving for authority. The person invested with an official appointment is committed to one thing only: keeping his position at any cost. And what about religious people? Politics is showbiz for the ugly; religion is politics for the introverted.

The artist can denounce this state of affairs, because she is by definition the stranger, the foreigner. *Kuenstler* was the term assigned in the middle Ages to able artisans and individuals with no fixed abode or permanent occupation who lived outside the hierarchy of social and economic values, strangers who aroused suspicion and were perceived as embodiment of the devil.

The artist does not revel in the moral superiority of one unable to commit the wrongs of the man of power. Rather than saying, "Thank God I am not capable of such greed or cruelty," he exclaims, "Mankind is capable of doing even this". A voice destined to echo in the desert, forever at the margins of traditional history because the person in power, as the hegemonic nation, are forever unable to admit defeat or weakness.

Horror is rarely visible in all its malevolence, dotted as it is with trivially respectful deeds, its steady plea to reality and circumstance. Ethics is reborn as individual thought and deed, as dialogue with oneself, at variance with conscience and self-examination, that dull interior survey of restrictions dictated by the super-ego. It is instead akin to a dialogue with one's own *daimon*. He who can talk to his own *daimon* can talk to another: this is precisely how thought comes into being. But thought becomes atrophied where there is no silence, no reflection and no trust in otherness. Totalitarian societies create a general atmosphere of mistrust, and democratic late-capitalist societies pollute silence through the proliferation of pseudo-information.

The Ontology Compulsion

The opposite of ethics is not evil but *monolatry*, the one-dimensional interpretation of a subject who avoids the precarious and horizontal response to infinity and resorts instead to ready-made answers offered by totalizing systems.

Evil is not apprehended here univocally as psychotic foray by external and internal forces inside the ego's domain, but as a wide Dionysian dimension full of creative possibilities, a dimension seeking manifestation, mastery and refinement (the assimilation of Apollonian traits) after its initial disruptive phase. These possibilities are, however, considerably reduced if ethics become constrained by religious dictates. More simply put, unless we access ethics via our inevitable human wound, no significant transformation can take place. Without shared acknowledgement of the common wound (which is the essence of communication), the super-ego will adorn itself with 'spiritual' maxims leaving our armour intact, and our heart unaffected.

The average bourgeois individual – stressed out by work, beleaguered by risible gratifications, frightened by illnesses which suddenly struck him or a loved one – turns to psychotherapy and meditation in search of relief and consolation, the promise of some happiness, or some kind of integration. He cannot accept the wound but pines away trying to outflank it and medicate it. In some spiritual path or other he will find a catechism, a method aimed at avoiding that sense of groundlessness sneaking into his life. He will accept bargain metaphysics, purchase any merchandise offering an outlet from anguish and an impending sense of futility. But even

18

though he might have the necessary tools and discipline to own a sophisticated metaphysics, it won't make any difference, and that's because metaphysics itself is an absurdity. Sure enough, a particular idea finds popularity for a while by fortuitous combination with truthfulness but its fortune is brief and subject to change.

In this context the definition of philosophy changes: it is no longer compulsion to ontology but an effort to describe living-and-dying and via the necessary artificiality of contemplation acclimatizing oneself to the descent into phenomenal existence. What redeems philosophy is precisely the gratuitousness of its enquiry, its proximity to wonder and the *wisdom-that-knows-groundlessness*. The common sense of philosophic wisdom is a rare quality: the religious person will say it is a gift from the deity, and the artist might say it is a poetic gesture.

Meditation, in this context, can be understood as being able to appreciate the mystery of the everyday, as the activity of a healthy organism who can afford gratitude. In this perspective we could reconcieve *nihilism* as the denigration of the everyday, its reduction to "nothing" (*nihil*); as the hijacking of the everyday's inherent meaning for the sake of a spiritual ideal.

In Praise of the Everyday

I call ethics the appreciation of the everyday, as a tribute to those thinkers who have affirmed the primacy of ethics above ontology, because *ethics has no essence; its essence is to disturb essences*. Its identity is absence of identity, and its task is that of undoing identity. Radical ethics, understood as unconditional praise of the everyday, annoys the vainglory of being and the melodrama of nothingness. To be or not to be: was there ever a more histrionic question?

To foundational reveries we invariably return, like a pilgrim who weeps while recalling the homeland. Contemporary humanistic psychology managed at first to somehow evade that loving cage of Platonic union by bravely entering the widowhood of individuation, by opening a clearing in the jungle of multiplicity. Then, suddenly mystified and perplexed by the overwhelming presence of infinity, it began to trace its steps back to the Platonic comfort-zone. It did so by manufacturing notions aimed at assuaging a powerful need for consolation, in the attempt to overcome both an innate sense of inferiority towards psychoanalysis and a fear of ineffectiveness compared to the hard facts of cognitive-behaviourism.

Notions of "relational depth" and "configurations of self" thus began to emerge in the heart of a radical tradition such as the person-centred approach, a clinical philosophy inspired by Carl Rogers, a practitioner and theorist who had refuted the notion of depth (product of a belief in the unconscious), the Cartesian notion of a separate and self-sufficient psychic apparatus, as well as the Freudian idea of psyche as a mechanism made up of parts.

Because inhabiting exteriority for any length of time is hard, the subject seeks (tragically, as well as comically) to find its way back into the womb of nostalgic union. It is disappointing to register how the experimental, falsifiable notions of humanistic psychology gradually solidify into dogma. This is further confirmation perhaps of how psychology and psychotherapy have substituted for religion, seeming to express nostalgia for a lost deity. It is clearance sale of the everyday to make room for the sublime, substituting therapeutic rigour for mysticism or scientism.

Non-Dialogical Conversations

Recognition of otherness goes well beyond the rhetoric of dialogue, according to which the subject edits the living narrative and the interlocutor becomes a text to be read and interpreted. This outlook shows faith in the story, in an imaginary meaning which must be uncovered or at least narrated in a different way. The dialogical/inter-subjective approach promotes conversation, accessed via a stance of not-knowing, yet does not acknowledge the fact that dialogue is at heart a way of placating the anxiety of intrinsic duality and contradiction present in every person. Discourse inevitably tends towards seduction, argument, condescension, by means of attraction, revulsion, and indifference, in the attempt to reassure ourselves that the other is *similar* to us. There are essentially two modes of dialogue: dialectic and non-dialectic (or poetic). The dialectic mode divides further into three sub-groups: objective, inter-subjective, and immediate.[3]

(1) In the *objective* dimension, the other is perceived as object of scientific observation, whether as an aggregate of instincts and drives, a carrier of symptoms, or a subject to be re-programmed and re-educated. This dimension is normative, invariably in tune with the demands of the market and of the dominant ideology, and is indifferent to the real needs of an individual.

(2) In the *inter-subjective* dimension, the other is perceived as another self, different yet one with whom I am able to establish contact via some form of primary identity. A key exponent of this modality in later years is Stolorow, in turn influenced by Gadamer, a thinker who has perhaps ignored the defrauding influence of bourgeois ideology. Free communication is of course a fantasy, and to suppose otherwise makes Gadamer's method, which largely inspired the inter-subjective view, essentially conservative.

Otherness is certainly not an unusual discovery – western thought often addressed it, yet each time it takes the other into consideration it regards the other as other from *me*. For Husserl only the domain of the ego is original; for Heidegger only the backdrop of being justifies interest in the other.

(3) In attempting fusion with the other in the *immediate* encounter, the self forget distance. Intensity, authenticity, and loss of self are all key elements here. The otherness of the other is lost in such fusion, in itself a form of spiritual and existential bypass. The singularity of the other is sacrificed at several altars: new age mysticism, established religions, Heidegger's neutral Being.

The three dialectic sub groups just described share a common tendency, a compulsion even, to unity: the objective analyst, the inter-subjective humanist, and the empathic spiritualist unanimously attempt to reduce the unease they feel in finding themselves face-to-face with otherness. All three miss the key element of every encounter: *separation*. Is this compulsion to unity beneficial? Among the synonyms of unity we find: accord, totality, harmony, unison, conformity. Unity is therefore harmony but also conformity.

Among all illusions, believing that I *understand* another is perhaps the most insidious. Desire to know and to appropriate the other belongs to the art of war; it belongs to politics and diplomacy. The desire to become one with the other belongs to the Platonic nostalgia of union and to the flight of transcendence.

21

The space between self and other is not only to be maintained, but cultivated: we need to know how to actively renounce our need to understand the other.

The non-dialectic mode is, on the other hand, poetic; it does not aspire to union but fully recognizes the foreignness of the other. Here discourse approximates poetry, for it willingly loses its inclination towards unity and veers towards infinity. The abyss between the two shores is not filled, explained, or concealed but is felt and recognized.

Anarchist Ethics

From its inception, psychology attempted to imitate the natural sciences. Yet natural sciences have totalized the infinity of the world by organizing it, indexing and itemizing its features with the aim of exercising mastery over it. Psychology has similarly striven to classify human beings but this is an arduous task for humans resist totalization. Nevertheless technology continues in its attempts to seduce psychology, and an outcome of this is the cynicism of action, the efficient manipulation which succeeds in subjugating even humanists, psychotherapists, and philosophers, effectively turning the subtle art of psychology into a tool of control and acquiescence.

The alternative could be seeing the human sciences as an expression of ethics, and more specifically of an ethics which, following the example of Levinas and Ellul, I do not hesitate to call *anarchic*. The ascendancy of the other on the subject, Levinas teaches us, *interrupts* the subject, leaves him speechless. In this motion, political and poetic at the same time, one begins to glimpse a valid alternative to the dominant view dictated by the rule of law. At its core lies the obligation towards the other rather than alienation, and this occurs through embodied presence. The latter is not to be confused with the notion of concreteness, which is only the flipside of abstraction, part of a sterile configuration finding its apotheosis in neuro-scientism, a discipline which variously drawing inspiration from Spinoza, primary relations in infancy, and the inherent sociability of human beings, ends up reducing consciousness to the working of neurotransmitters, and the mind to the brain.

A third way out of the concreteness/abstraction impasse is

expressed by a neurologist whose insights preceded by some decades Gestalt psychology as well as the *organismic* perspective of humanistic psychology: Kurt Goldstein. An exceptionally rare and original case of physician/philosopher, Goldstein identified such an alternative in what he calls the sphere of *immediacy*.

Of I–Thou as Accident

The definition of the human being has undergone several metamorphoses across the centuries: from creature to monad; from monad to simulacrum. More recently the trajectory from late-Romanticism to modernism helped create a new artefact, the bourgeois soul, a soul even more powerful because widespread and mimetic. It has been possible once for philosophers to assert a natural trust in any encounter with others, even strangers, and to say that mistrust towards strangers occurs only in extreme circumstances. It has been possible to state that human life cannot even be sustained without this fundamental trust. Yet to trust means to expose oneself, and if one is not capable of trusting in this way, conflict follows, or the surrogate of conflict, i.e. moralizing projection, accusation and the *perverse intimacy* of hatred. Wounded, with amorous fury (love *in absentia*, but love nevertheless), one sets to obliterate any prospect of reconciliation and proceeds to open the gates of hell and of dissociation.

Is it still possible, in the era of global conformity and universal tedium, to trust the incessant renewal of life? Only this trust can allow otherness to emerge anew from the entanglements and restrictions which bind it. Human existence refuses to be reduced to an assortment of past behaviours. Each individual seeks to disentangle herself from the chains of determinism, asserting her right to appeal. Each individual wants to be seen under the uncertain and prodigious light of a new day. To each individual we must allow the redemption of new words and new deeds. Can natural trust in the incessant renewal of life win over the tendency to reify existence? Perhaps the two movements are equally necessary, like Eros and Thanatos, freedom and determinism. Perhaps, like Eros and Thanatos, they are complementary. Without a wholly gratuitous trust in the other, communication cannot take place, because communication needs abandon and risk. But we cannot abide in this realm for very long: the *I–Thou* dimension, without which we cannot call ourselves humans, is miraculous, i.e. accidental; it cannot be manufactured at will. It is naïve to think, as some contemporary psychotherapy does, that one may access this domain simply via the creation of necessary and sufficient conditions. These conditions – contact, congruence, empathy, unconditional positive regard and so forth – no doubt create the atmosphere, making the room ready for the guest's visit. But the arrival is uncertain, the time of arrival unknown, and it's not in our power to alter any of these circumstances. Strenuous advocates of inter-subjectivity easily forget that for Buber the *I–Thou* encounter is a rare occurrence rather than the easy outcome of facile utopia.

From child psychology we learn how interactions of adults with children greatly affect the infants's psyche, but we tend to forget the equally powerful impact subsequent interactions between adults have on our world and our destiny. The reason we ignore this might be twofold: first of all we are not aware of the most obvious occurrences; secondly, it would weigh heavily upon us to consider how much our actions indent the life of others.

What is This?

To pathology, i.e. to the most acute forms of human distress, we owe our study of *psyche*, a study grounded in biology, understood as study of living beings rather than adherence to the alleged objectivity of the bio-medical model. Grounding in biology ensures abandonment of anthropocentrism as well as zoo-morphism. In this way we come to acknowledge the wider domain of *psyche*, another name describing organismic experience unconstrained by biologism. The link with biology ensures embodiment, being-in-the-world, and distance from the clutches of Platonic idealism. In the symptoms emerging from the organism one recognizes attempts at solution, organismic responses to distress rather than isolated expressions of localized damage.

Awareness of the body and of phenomena does not lead us back to materialist determinism or to denying the unknowability of existence. On the contrary, it prompts us to anchor our life practice in the body; it also invites us to *look again*, and with a fresh attitude, to those things which materialism takes for granted. We become then aware of *lived life* yet alert to its unfathomable nature. This constitutes our anchor and compass, keeping us grounded yet open and equanimous when all around there is consternation in the face of uncertainty and doubt.

The incompleteness of the modernist project and the wide gaps left unfilled by science do not trouble us. We know that modernism had only two options left: run on empty or remain stranded in the proliferation of positivist pseudo-solutions.

Since Descartes, and via the logical positivism of the twentieth century, the modernist project has underlined the central role of epistemology as well as the need for adequate interpretations with regard to the relation of the subject with assumed reality – with a harmonious, even *fair* reality: these now have all the hallmarks of foolish ambitions, emanations of that religious thought which modernism had confidently believed defeated.

Brilliant and many-sided, the modernist project was destined to fail. How long can we immerse a bowl in the river stream and, observing it later diligently within four walls, believe that we are examining the river itself? The stream flows on, ungraspable and unpredictable. The river cannot go back to the source. Who suffers, afflicted by ontological insecurity, is bound to perceive with greater intensity what most of us avoid, neutralize or passively accept. The sufferer wants to exit the river of life because it leads to death. He wants to find refuge in ritual and compulsion, trying to evade the stream of living-and-dying.

The psychotherapist has a thankless task: to urge the client back to the river of life thus renewing the promise of death. Even more thankless is the task of the philosopher: remembering the initial commitment to remain attentive of the delicate labour of death. *Memento mori* – because this is what it is all about, "remember that you will die", but this time, one hopes, without the shrill disparaging overtones of religion but as a tonic of remembrance urging us towards life and tragic joy.

Even the Buddhist practitioner will have to recognize sooner or later the centrality of such unadorned awareness. Facing an object, one spontaneously asks: "What is this?" and if one has a philosophical mind one may ask: "What is its essence?" Yet both questions are artificial, induced by the arbitrary removal of the object from the stream of becoming. The same question *what is this?* is a *koan* in the Korean Zen tradition, and it does not refer to the object or the subject but addresses becoming itself, seized in the totality of present experiencing. This leads us to a panoramic awareness anchored in the body – to an awareness of the present when the present is no more.

Loyal to Phenomenology

From the fertile soil of phenomenology Husserl affirmed a transcendental ego while Heidegger placed his faith in the neutrality of a being that would automatically host the attributes of concern. Levinas opened up phenomenology to ethics and alterity, thus re-formulating the basis of ethics itself, no longer subordinated to social, moral or religious structures or to psychological functions but understood as obligation to the other. Recognizing this obligation does not require expertise nor particular refinement but the willingness to lean out, to come into contact with otherness and leaving behind one's place in the sun. In leaning out towards alterity the self is born for the first time. It abandons the chrysalis of solipsism where it lived until now. Prompted by desire, the individual dares an intimacy with foreignness and abandons the self of metaphysics, social consensus and totalizing morality. It abandons subjectivism and welcomes the individuality that emerges in the shared space, the sphere of immediacy – not a mystical dimension but the everyday itself, a dimension shared and temporarily de-colonized from logical and dialectical interpretations and from the acquisitive project of ipseity. One gains access to this sphere via a voluntary surrender, a momentary suspension, or *epoché* – acted without fear of losing oneself.

Unless it is a suffering organism, this act of surrender does not imply catharsis or release of tension. The sick organism looks for release of pain and preservation of its basic functions: in this sense the preservation instinct is to be considered a form of pathology. The natural tendency of the organism is instead directed towards *actualization*: the will to become is will to power, will to create and expand, to join life's aspiration to overcome itself. Animated by desire, we experience ourselves more fully as active and desiring persons, rather than passive receptors of blind drives (as classic psychoanalysis had believed) or provoked by lack and absurdity (as existentialism had believed).

Ethic sensibility demands a radical reformulation of those notions which, ratified by medicine, psychology and religion, have now fossilized into dogmas. Think, for instance, of suffering, sanctified by religious rhetoric, ennobled by Buddhist teachings, and justified by the secular theodicy of medicine and psychology. The justification of the other's suffering can never be legitimized by an existentially and politically committed radical ethics, one that is animated by a sense of justice and by the refusal to accept the suffering of the oppressed. It is also an *anarchic* stance, i.e. a refusal of ontology, of the autarchy implied by *archè*, hence recognition of the ascendancy of alterity, commitment to abstain from prevarication in the inevitable disparity of *any* encounter. Ethics understood in this way is more important than religion and spirituality and also, as William James would say, more important then psychology itself.

Another area coming under scrutiny is the *law*, for a radical ethics dares to conceive law outside Hobbesian influence and outside utilitarianism. The ethical obligation precedes sin and alienation – an obligation, it must be stressed, which can and must evade the constriction of the super-ego.

And what about psychology? Is psychology possible outside neurology and neuroscience? An embodied psychology, one that has assimilated the teachings of Nietzsche and Merleau-Ponty, won't need to abdicate to a reductivism explaining away psyche via brain waves. Is a psychology possible which is able to de-construct and de-center the self?

Ethics has gone through different phases: from the critique of Cartesian subjectivity to the affirmation of the everyday as prime morality, and via the gradual recognition that an adequate investigation of human existence needs to go beyond self-preoccupation. It has affirmed de-centred states of self, states of radical absence and passivity such as simplicity, patience, humility. All of these are anomalies in contemporary psychology because, often driven by envy towards the natural sciences, psychology parodied its procedures and

27

sought in human vicissitudes that same natural order described by these sciences. In spite of the fact that human beings continue to blunt such quantifications and that they do not behave like the docile subjects positivism wishes them to be, each new development in psychology straight-facedly renews the technologization of therapeutic intervention, confirming a compulsion towards utilitarian functionalism and a philistine pragmatism which is not only devoid of imagination but is also centred on the manipulation of the subject, on its re-integration in the world of productivity.

Radical philosophy, poetry and art need decades to be assimilated. We need decades to absorb the unfuthomable nature of the present. The now – *maintenant* in French – is what we hold in our hands, which nevertheless goes on evading us. We live the now guided by past notions, whereas the artist/philosopher describes the present, what eternally slips us by as sand between our fingers.

A New Psychology?

It is not possible to construct a new psychology inspired by ethics because ethics resists the creation of systems. From its perspective it is however possible to probe psychology well beyond its mere deconstruction, because in this case there is certainly something outside the text, namely otherness, the person to whom the text is implicitly addressed. The other – the tenderness and vulnerability of the face – cannot be incorporated within the subject's system because alterity is vertigo and vulnerability. The human dimension escapes the discursive dimension and responds to the caress, to the suffering without recompense of individuals who cross the waste land of mourning and guilt, of those who in these impossible regions find an apprenticeship capable of ennobling them more than their usual strategies of personal gain will ever be able to do.

At the same time one needs to extricate oneself from the quest for essence, affirming instead the passivity of an adequate response to otherness, far more urgent a task than grappling with the false problem of *Dasein*. One has to learn how to shiver in the wound which opens us to the existent, and find in the bewilderment and reverberation of that shiver the foundation of consciousness itself.

A Post-metaphysical Era

One might perhaps define post-modernity, with Bauman, as "modernity without illusions"[4]. What would the illusions be in this case? That it is possible to organize the chaos inherent to the human condition without belittling it; that there are metaphysical answers (able to provide a foundation to becoming) beyond the fallible and transient solutions we manufacture in contingent circumstances.

Paradoxically, ethics is possible only in our post-modern, post-metaphysical era, a time when morality is being re-personalized outside the ethical codes of religion and morality. The moral relativism which supposedly would follow is a necessary danger: human dignity inevitably implies arbitrariness and risk, and moral philosophy is internal rather than external work. The Kantian mystery of inner morality expands into the mystery of the concrete exteriority of the other towards whom I am obliged to respond, without recourse to the props of metaphysics or utilitarian self-interest. After all, what prompted Cain's murder were respectively metaphysics and self-interest: reacting to the injustice of an exclusivist God and eliminating a competitor.

Radical Respect

The triumph of technological *dis*information makes the practice of radical ethics even more urgent. The fragmentation produced by technology, while concealing the holistic nature of human life, has dissected the alleged moral atomism of the self, thus accelerating risks and responsibilities. In a mechanized world where it has become easier to blame a mechanism of which we are oblivious implements, the ethical response of the individual becomes weightier. An act of kindness – simple and genuine – becomes in our hyper-modern landscape automatically countercultural. In our neo-Machiavellian technological era, where the means are wholly removed from the end, anything interfering with the efficiency dogma becomes automatically other. In an era in which the individual himself is taken into consideration as emanation of *we* (a moral misrepresentation assisted by the grammatical injunction which sees in the I the mere singular of we), the real kindness of one individual becomes a radical act. One of these acts is respect, which potentially breaks the spell of mechanization. *Re-spect* means glancing twice, responding to the silent call and implicit demand of the other, with the second glance breaking our deference to the impersonal law. If answered, participation is established between two finite beings – this is the beginning of ethics.

I have explored with pupils and colleagues in classes and workshops the ethical demand as described by Scandinavian existential theology, in particular by Løgstrup. By listening attentively to the silent presence of the other, fundamental messages emerge, such as *Do not hurt me. Receive me. Receive my presence. Be kind to me. Listen. Look at me. Respect me.*

It is possible to break the spell of the dimension of *we* by listening to the other, and by listening to ourselves via the crystallization of what Rogers called an internal locus of evaluation. We must momentarily lose this *we*, the inorganic sum of aggregates and figures, and regain the *I* as ethical subject. Introspection might be a necessary phase on this path. Turning our glance inward does not lead to solipsism or the crystallization of the self, but allows us to observe its fluid and interdependent nature. Contemplation opens us to the *relative* existence of the self, rather than to solipsism. The experience of relativity (*śūnyatā*) is open, generous and makes us receptive to creativity. In the encounter with the other, from a space of risk and opportunity, the self emerges for the first time.

The Asymmetry of Encounter

An adequate response to the high demands of morality, idealized by religious injunctions and the categorical imperative, is actualized via radical ethics and the re-personalization of morality. Kantian insights had to wait two centuries to be embodied, and with this unexpected turn ethics contradicts the utopian principles of the Enlightenment and the otherworldly principles of religion. It also contradicts the notion of symmetry, taken for granted by dialogical thought (from Buber to Gadamer), affirming instead *asymmetry*.

To assume symmetric mutuality among beings means accepting neutrality, thus condoning the subject, preventing it from engaging with the anxiety of ethical choice, and depriving it of the existential dignity suggested by that choice. Being-with (*Mitsein*) on this neutral terrain means being *next* to the other; but only a face-to-face meeting properly initiates ethics. *Mitsein* merely re-assembles the dimension of *we*, a neutral locus where, huddled together around a deity and a nationality, we march in time, at war against otherness. On the other hand, being *for* the other implies ethical commitment, through which one is stripped of ipseity and re-emerges as an individual, i.e., one who is able to respond. Being-with can be regulated by the law. Being-for evades external injunctions and responds to interior necessity, the mystery of ethics inside me. 'Interior' is a descriptive term indicating a response to the presence of the other: the hospitality of one who recognizes the impossibility of residing anywhere and of being other than a guest. This is the hospitality of the *bodhisattva*, a being abandoned to infinite solitude hence able to respond to the inalienable solitude of the other. It is not society which makes us ethical people; adherence to social rules turns us into respectable bourgeois but not into *citizens* in the sense Hannah Arendt gives to the word, i.e. people able to feel solidarity and a civic responsibility beyond the call of duty.

From infancy the barrier to stimuli protects us, according to Freud, from the artillery of sensations; unfortunately the barrier ends up protecting us from others too. Freud's bio-poetic conjecture in *Beyond the Pleasure Principle* attributes a prominent role to protection, more important than the process of stimulus-reception itself. The organism builds an effective barrier against external stimuli but not against internal ones. It is to disowned aspects of the psyche that one would ascribe the notorious projections – notorious because every projection is projection of evil. This perspective is refuted by Daniel Stern,[5] and it is interesting to note that today it is universally accepted that the infant actively seeks stimuli rather than build a protection against the external world. A great consensus has gathered around the foundational character of the primary relationship, with inter-subjectivity as a key for comprehending, if not the human condition, at least what constitutes success in psychotherapy. It remains to be seen whether such enthusiasm towards inter-subjectivity honours or neglects the autonomy of the individual alongside the need for solitude and the equally crucial need for separation.

Inter-subjective psychology and psychotherapy has grasped for philosophical roots which might corroborate and add prestige to its affirmations. It has found teachers and inspirational figures, cutting and pasting from their philosophies what hypothetically substantiates a way of thinking. From Buber inter-subjective psychology has borrowed the notion of the *I–Thou*, conveniently forgetting that such elevated mode of relating is very rare, something that happens by chance or as an outcome of a long and hard discipline of risk and sacrifice, of respectively exposing oneself to the danger of intimacy and abandoning the infinite potentialities of a vibrant organism by crystallizing the creative act, accepting finitude and uniqueness. In ransacking Buber's rigorous ethics, inter-subjective psychologists have also neglected the central presence God has in his thought, without which his sanctification of human relations is but an empty simulacrum.

The question is not whether God exists or not, but whether the deity coincides with infinity and the de-centering of ipseity, with disorientation and a longing without object, with the indigent face demanding a response, or instead with totalizing interpretation, codification and personifications of norms, with a collective identity founded on violence and hatred of the other.

No such Thing as an equal Relationship

Psychology has borrowed from Gadamer[6] the notion of *fallibility*, which opens the possibility of genuine conversation and enquiry and signals the inevitability of prejudice within the interpretative process. However, in universalizing such a position, and in the transition from hermeneutics to psychotherapy (from the text to a living interlocutor), Gadamer omits the inherent disparity of any relationship, in this case of the helping relationship. The very term 'helping relationship' is dubious. It disregards the basic inequality and asymmetry of such encounter, as well as the falsifying influence of ideology. Gadamer's hermeneutics can be used as a valid model only when combined to active critique of any alleged 'spontaneous and direct communication' between individuals. A dialogue comes close to direct communication only when social, economic and political considerations support it, thus avoiding a slip into populism.

A Stranger to Myself

Ethics is necessarily beyond good and evil. According to the *Mumonkan*, a key text in Zen, to be concerned with good and evil amounts to coveting heaven and fearing hell; it amounts, in other words, to a servile attitude. The life of virtue, bearer of happiness – Aristotle's *eudaimonia* – in this context means paying attention to one's own *daimon*, following one's vocation, obeying both fate and character. Actualizing is not actualizing a self, by its nature devoid of intrinsic existence, but following the *organism*'s tendency towards actualization. Kurt Goldstein and later humanistic psychology have taught us that actualization coincides with a positive stance of cooperation and active contribution to society. It is however necessary to acquire an inner locus of evaluation at variance with tribal mentality and the ideology of the herd of which the self is an introjected fragment. This is even more valid in a post-modern era which has sanctioned the end of ideology while effectively bowing down to bourgeois ideology.

The primal soil must become alien to us, and this is not enough: we must become strangers to ourselves; in such estrangement a space opens, an invitation to sift through the cultural contents which constituted us. Detached from tribal ideology, having followed a path of individuation, of voluntary descent and exile, the individual goes back to the human community in order to offer a contribution.

Such process is dance, apprenticeship and initiation to both *phronēsis* and *sophia*, to ordinary acumen and the wisdom of the sages, to common sense and the sublime. In Dharma teachings we find a direct correlation between these two aspects of wisdom (*prajñā*): they are two faces of the same coin, emerging as immediate response to conditionality.

Assimilation of the Dharma in the West has taken place via German idealism, American transcendentalism and various ideologies of repentance; such categories have coloured western Dharma from the beginning. But *prajñā* must be *digested*, the great *Ch'an* master Huang-Po would say, in a daily practice at the centre of which is *zazen*, meditation without an object. Virtues (*paramitas*) are apprehended and assimilated rather than acquired by the will. The latter is an attribute of the self, which will inevitably declare its own moral uprightness. In the same way, Buddhist precepts are neither injunctions nor methods aimed at spiritual awakening, but themselves manifestations of Buddha-nature.

Among the consequences of the death of God is the misunderstanding of ethics as transaction and regulation as well as the loss of those characteristics, inherited from Hellenism, which see ethics as cultivation of character, care of self via the virtuous disposition arising from listening to one's *daimon* – from courage, humility and compassion (attributes of the *instant*) and by their subsequent organization into morality, loyalty and justice (attributes of the *interval*).

The individual cannot survive long in the instant, in the *I–Thou* dimension of authentic communication, vulnerability and risk. Nor can she survive if inhabiting only the *interval*, the domain of codified law and adherence to social norms. In the first case, one would burn as a meteor in the summer sky; in the second, one would end up embalmed in the Museum of Respectability. These are both caricatures of ethics and destroy the poetic nature of virtue, a goddess in continuous flight, a goddess who exists in flight.

The domain of law sees the triumph of institutionalized bad faith, what we call social life, existence organized in accordance with complex strategies of non-encounter, a network of missed opportunities. Since it is not feasible to avoid stumbling upon, or having to deal with, the stranger and the foreigner, we elaborate complex rituals of non-encounter in order to keep alive our claim as moral beings. There are of course instances when such convoluted farce is pushed aside to make way to barbarism and primitivism in all its guises.

The ethical imperative is therefore not apprehended (Kant) or contemplated (Plato) and *then* applied. It is created in the instant, when I perceive the face in front of me in a face-to-face encounter. It is not an act of will but of gratuitous convergence between contingency and the individual's openness to experience; it is the working of grace, or a miracle. Or, if one does not wish to use religious language, it is *poetry*. For example, in the gratuitous act of forgiveness, one perceives the instant, the threshold where the linear trajectory of time acquires meaning for the first time (and it is always the first time). Rational forgiveness can excuse only what is excusable and in doing so demonstrates the moral superiority of those who forgive. Forgiveness born out of poetic vision forgives the unforgivable. One often ends up loving the person one has forgiven.

Jankélévitch[7] unmasks the various kinds of inauthentic forgiveness we use in order to adorn our behaviour: we may forgive out of calculation; we absolve the reprobate hoping the future will vindicate us. We may forgive impelled by optimism and arrogance; prey to spiritual concupiscence, we want to redeem the guilty, the lost soul who will be transformed through contact with our immeasurable goodness. We may forgive strategically: *odium amore expugnare* (Spinoza).

If, on rare occasions, we are caught red-handed by grace, we quickly excuse ourselves and sing a utilitarian praise in the language of business. We imitate Pascal who persuades the atheist to a probabilistic faith.

Perhaps there is no such thing as authentic forgiveness and if there is, it is a form of love – but not the coquettish or 'romantic' kind with a small *r*. The minstrel churns out sonnets and pop songs but he is truly in love with himself and with his own noble soul radiating garrulous tunes. And yet one can be overwhelmed by love, when the finitude of the other floods the heart with melancholy and kindness, with the sweetness of Virgil's muse, pre-Christian, i.e. free from the bad taste of exclusive, fanatic love, free from the flattering seduction of the immortal soul and its melodramatic contests of redemption and sin. Virgilian *pietas*, like *bodhicitta*, is asymmetric; the lover is disinterested, her song is flame and caress. She laughs at expiation and karma, at a notion of justice measured by the scales in the market place; she pokes fun at the 'eye for an eye', at the deterministic barbarism present in every religion. *Pietas* goes beyond mere gratitude, which can be a result of obligation, closely related to ingratitude and all too often coated with religious zeal.

If forgiveness is born out of a computation made within the domain of the *interval*, then by forgiving we run the risk of appearing sublime. But forgiveness can be also, as Stendhal has it, an act of *crystallization,* of transfiguration of love which turns an ordinary lover into a genius of the heart. Transfiguration takes place in the domain of the *instant* and prompts us to act ethically. Later we will look for motives and guiding principles. However, one who lives poetically forgives, for he takes for granted what Nietzsche calls the *innocence of*

35

becoming. We accept the other. Acceptance accepts because it accepts. A *bodhisattva* does not wait for a hypothetic enlightenment; she acts right now, i.e. in the domain of the instant. Love loves because it loves. Light years from the solipsistic melodrama of repentance, forgiveness hurls us towards exteriority and through its impact we are instructed and educated. Education is not maieutics, a pre-existing interior monologue which the skilled Socratic interlocutor helps us extract from the imaginary source of inner life. It manifests instead through our encounter with alterity and the unknowability of the other.

The Impersonality of Ancient Wisdom

Who knows, Kant asks in *Fundamental Principles of the Metaphysics of Morals*, if there has ever been a single virtuous deed in the history of humanity. A very valid question: virtue does not belong to the domain of ipseity. Forgiveness and disinterested love are not attributes of identity. Compassion is an attribute congenial to a deity, an apparition which escapes us while it appears, an apparition appearing in relation. Forgiveness appears in relation and is different from the clemency of the Stoics and the generous benevolence of those who forgive and love impersonally, like a king blindly distributing his gifts to faceless subjects. Ancient wisdom is often impersonal and finds an unexpected correlative in the quest of the post-modern neophyte seeking lofty refuge from the samsaric tumult of this valley of tears. Both the exhausted metropolitan dweller and the solipsistic Internet surfer seek *ataraxy* and a form of indifference mistaken for equanimity; they seek a balm, *any* balm to soothe the multiple injuries of the post-modern condition.

The generic philanthropy preached by the Stoics, the abstract benevolence of those who love the forest but ignore the tree, the mysticism of contemporary 'trans-personal' discourse which bypasses the person without having first understood her, the transcendental neo-Zen that forgets the self without having studied it first: is such thirst for transcendence an escape from the human condition?

Reverberation, not Resonance

Ethics is not possible without an awareness of impermanence. It precedes philosophy, science, and religion; these are concerned with being, facticity, and eternity. Without awareness of impermanence, art and love are not possible. Everything changes incessantly, including the subject observing the change, including consciousness itself.

Time is crucial in ethics. The unmotivated act of forgiveness confirms becoming, that fleeting dimension against which philosophy erects systems, religion builds temples, and governments build prison houses. By accepting becoming one accepts the fragmentary and ephemeral nature of the self. Exteriority then reaches us as *reverberation*, and no longer as resonance. Resonance, a fashionable term, has at its centre the self, who brings back to itself exteriority's genuine impact; it turns every encounter into a tourist excursion. Reverberation has the other at its centre; by being receptive to the concentric circles of sound radiating from the other the self is potentially transformed. The centrality of the other and the centrality of becoming are intimately connected.

Nevertheless they do not exclude memory: loyalty to becoming is not abstract ludic spontaneity. Openness to becoming (appearance, impermanence) is even more powerful when supported by memory. Memory (that is, imagination) enriches experience; it constitutes the backdrop where the unrepeatable expression of the instant becomes vivid to an implausible degree. We are accomplices of becoming, rooted in a faculty, memory, equally subject to change. Imagination re-enacts distant memories – a shift in present experience modifies memory itself.

Rancour resists becoming, it freezes the person who has injured us and does not accept alterations or the fact that the other is part of the river of living-and-dying. Forgiveness embraces becoming, dissolves the alleged solidity of self and other, and meets life without unnecessary burdens. One learns to forget, to practice the discipline of dynamic oblivion – thus dispersing the jaded phantom of rancour kept alive by superstitions. By dissipating our rancour, the memory of the injury suffered is also dissipated. By feeding our resentment, we instead fire at the void, for the object we aim at has moved on.

And if love for a phantom is by definition bewitched, rancour is doubly bewitched: it is not only outmoded but harmful.

The path of individuation does not follow the conventional trajectory of maudlin homecoming. Coming back to oneself is marked by resonance: an external sound is assimilated and neutralized. With reverberation, on the other hand, alterity reaches me whilst keeping intact its poetic force, its disquieting and transformative potential. Here there is no answer but listening, the fluid discipline gently corroding the obstinacy of ipseity.

In desire without object or aim, the excursion beyond the borders of ipseity is valid only in so far as it is reverberation of alterity. Similarly, individuation is rupture, widowhood, and loss. Exile is the adventure – devoid of illusion – nearing the exiled to the fleetingness of our condition.

Amnesty, not Amnesia

A descent into becoming brings about ambivalent results: by accepting imperfection and impermanence, we experience some degree of solace hence we think that we are safe from dangers. Yet suffering is now felt more directly, for time is regenerative as well as deadly. The sick organism slowly comes back to health, and the wounded heart heals with time, yet time inexorably leads to old age, a dimming of vitality, and eventually death. It is difficult to have complete trust in becoming, for it seduces us yet ends up killing us.

Awareness of the dialectics of becoming may encourage us to accept its ordeal by responding rather than submissively taking its blows. Passive forgiveness is born out of a one-sided perception of transience; it is apathy, more *amnesia* than *amnesty* as Jankélévitch reminds us. In contrast, a forgiveness that takes on becoming is addressed to the other, conscious of his mutability, of death-in-life, of the changes the other undergoes. This type of forgiveness is therefore different from the one conferred by the spiritual egotist who capitalizes a grievance he has been subjected to in order to beautify his noble soul.

Time and oblivion alone cannot heal us from resentment. "Of course I forgive you – people say – what you did was such a long time ago". But it is I, not time itself, who must be able to forgive –

instantly, for no reason, and despite myself. I make a decision outside the domain of will, because will by its very nature belongs to the ego. My decision is therefore a gift; by offering it, I defy psychological processes and biological evolution; my gift contradicts contemporary dogmas of process and growth.

Acting ethically implies a rupture. It is an act of creation rather than growth; it is the implausible, what has not occurred or been seen before. *Jamais vu*, rather than *déjà vu*: perplexity, doubt, wonder, experiencing that which cannot be replaced. Ethical action is the deed of a great artist who disappears into her creation. It is an act against nature, opposed to territoriality and the tendency towards violent crystallization of identity on which natural and religious principles are based. It is also opposed to the conformism of what is commonly deemed natural. Apprehended in this way, ethics is art rather than morality. It is anti-real, as any art worth its salt is anti-real, including realist art.

Socrates neither forgives nor is resentful with the Athenian tribunal but says "No one hurts another knowingly". Is such imper-sonality *ethical*? Ancient wisdom overlooks the finiteness of the other, elevates the injured party so high that the injury cannot reach him: it is a hygienic expedient and also a denigration of human feelings. In Zen sanghas it is fashionable to speak of 'idiot compassion' but in disparaging paternalistic piety one can easily overlook the wound implicit in every form of communication and summarily dispose of a dimension deemed 'relative' hence secondary.

Ethics go beyond the cognitive forgiveness and the intellectual conversion one might experience in the presence of a teacher who bestows nuggets of wisdom in accord with a particular idea of the good. We find an invitation to the fractional understanding of intel-lectual conversion in Leibniz, who exhorts the individual, limited monad, to harmonize with the cosmos. We also find it in Spinoza, who invites us to befriend our neighbour and above all befriend ourselves. We find it in the New Testament where we are told that both the onlookers and the assassins "know not what they are doing" and therefore refuse to believe the teachings of an ordinary man not clad in divine or regal garments. We find a call for conversion in Hellenism, under the guise of self-mastery – rendered by Nietzsche as *self-overcoming*.

It is certainly a conversion, recognition of the complexity and multiplicity of the psyche, this discovery of a need for mastery no longer based on the monadic self but on individuality. Such conversion is secular and symbolic. It is poetic even before being religious and it transmutes intellectual understanding into embodiment.

Vertigo is a sign that conversion has taken place, akin to the sense of danger we feel when we abandon false security. A trustworthy method for applying the flame of intellectual gaze without the smoke of the ego is *suspension of judgement*, suggested by Sextus Empiricus, and known as *epoché*. It remains to be seen if such suspension heralds Husserlian transcendence, if its aim is *ataraxia* or if it is essentially an act of love (of radical passivity, the desire for a knowledge which for Levinas is *love*), an act whose implications are, in a Sartrean sense, political.

In any case, an act of renunciation opens the possibility of love and disentangles morality from the talons of the super-ego. The intuition of an essence (true or imaginary) goes through empathy as well as a knowledge that is not-knowing. The more she loves, the less the lover knows her beloved. Hers is a state of profound ignorance which intentionally creates a distance between the self and the autonomy/unknowability of the other. A required and deliberate blindness – opposed to the lucidity or rancour and the perverse intimacy of hatred. Hatred engulfs the subject with the blinding light of interrogation. In dissecting it, it extracts a confession, learns trivial or incriminating details, but deviates from the subtle music which animates it and makes it part of the river of existence. Such knowledge kills the other and builds in its place a simulacrum to be moulded at leisure. Not-knowing is instead inspired by Eros, son of Poros and Penia: poor, he inhabits need and desire but is also brave, intense, and a great hunter. To Eros we owe the crucial descent from the peak of impersonal wisdom down to personal love, the everyday, immanence, the imperfection of becoming. Such descent is an act of folly for it loves what is not lovable or worthy of love. It is a ruinous fall which nevertheless gives meaning to our existence and averts us from a tyrannical search for happiness. It is a scandalous love in as much as it snubs the alleged wisdom of impersonality and sustains a difficult encounter with the other. Jankélévitch prefers resentment to passive oblivion because in it we still find seriousness, depth and a commitment of the heart, the refusal to find solace in bland rec-onciliation. On the other hand, cultivating resentment means refusing an encounter with the other and the recognition of one's own inferiority.

We must then consider cases in which solidarity towards the oppressed turns into the misguided obligation to respect the hierar-chies and prejudices of that particular group. Within oppressed communities too alterity is denied and privileges remain unchanged. A radical respect of otherness needs to affirm exile, absence of dwelling, and to articulate a refusal of integration and identity. This is because within the painful and difficult condition of exile lies hidden the potential freedom from the false need of identity and nationality, as well as from having and being. Unavoidable within global capitalism, exile – forced or voluntary – asserts the drifting nature of the human condition.

This implies full acceptance of the consequences of the death of God. A thorough-going secularism refuses any shadow of God, including scientism, faith in conventional politics and the idolatrous practices of happiness. After Hegel, secularism has been associated with faith in history, understood as metaphysical source and explana-tory origin through which we interpret events in an evolutionary and deterministic key. It would be interesting to re-consider in this context the teachings of Vico and Gramsci, both advocates of non-messianic, non-totalizing yet emancipatory conceptions of history.

One of the outcomes of a thorough-going secularism is the ques-tioning of identity as the last legacy of a God long deceased. Abandoning voluntarily the false notion of identity is also, in my view, the primary focus of Dharma practice. Buddhism – without beliefs or prejudices – is a path of premeditated disorientation and must not be confused with the current fashionable search for happi-ness.

To abandon one's place in the sun, to dispose of one's own iden-tity – and with it of the very notion of identity – implies opening up to the polyphony within oneself and within the culture one happens to belong. What we leave behind is universalism – always dictated by hegemonic forces – and its fabrication of ideal syntheses of disparate societies through the bypassing of specificity. What we leave behind is also that convenient love of humanity which easily

forgets the fundamental asymmetry of social and political relationships. We move beyond the evolutionary transcendentalism which
imagines gathering and integrating insights from several spiritual
traditions evading their anthropologic, mythical, as well as socio-
economic particularity.

Who can nowadays embrace exile and nomadism, radical secularism and a conscious refusal of identity and integration? First of all
those who, forced into such a position by western democracies, feudal
regimes and the values imposed by nation-states cannot but actively
accept this state of affairs. Then artists, anti-dynastic intellectuals, all
those who are disloyal to populist notions of tribal belonging and
refuse abstract allegiances to an ethnic or a political group. The
artist's role is to break vast national, cultural and trans-cultural identities, to unmask the universalism of the powerful and reveal the
pseudo-organic nature of any social, political and national group. The
role of the artist and of the intellectual is to affirm individuality, not
as a return to solipsism and the dubious universality of reason, but as
re-evaluation of the notions of critique, originality, and self-reflec-
tion – to reshape identity through adherence to movements and
people who noticeably suffer the barbarism and cruelty of hegemonic
groups.

Loyalty to the oppressed is not dogmatic allegiance to a would-be
messianic class but readiness to support those without any support.
For a bourgeois artist or intellectual this necessarily implies *renunciation* of one's own privileges and of the very notions of identity and
power.

Bourgeois Entropy

A bourgeois ethics is a contradiction in terms. Ethics requires being
able to recognize experiences external to the subject, whereas bourgeois life is by definition centred on the self and defined by the
incapacity to understand and appreciate what unfolds outside the
precinct of its possessions.

The global uniformity which started after the second world war
made of the bourgeois ideal a universal model, an occurrence
Pasolini calls *bourgeois entropy*,[8] a term which describes well the

implosion of sheltered gratification – at once self-protection and self-incarceration, elevating *misanthropy* (hatred of the other) and *misology* (hatred of conversation) to a way of life. Ethics is not possible without encounter with otherness, because like musical performance and love – as if performed for the first time – it is not repetition but creation. As with music and love, in responding to otherness we remove the protective veil of dogma standing between ourselves and things, between ourselves and our actions. The individual surrenders ipseity involuntarily: the musician who touches the heart of the listener does so in spite of herself; sincere and painful regret befalls us and we suddenly feel the hurt we have caused another. One falls upon ethics, joy and ecstasy. One comes to love at last, but as a refugee. Ethics is a flower of the desert, not a greenhouse orchid. It is linked to suffering, to deep, tragic joy. Ethics, like philosophy, is an art.

There are those who deem philosophy a science, but philosophy is an art like poetry and the poetry of living. Philosophy must abandon ontological claims and the siren call of reason which turns humans into Titans. It has to do so in order to properly use reason rather than be used by it.

A world where religion still matters would be dependent on faith. The post-religious world inaugurated by Kant and the Enlightenment depended on reason. In our post-metaphysical world, the only choice left for philosophy is its own dissolution into ethics and aesthetics. Nothing obliges us to obey the *avid aspirations* and *irritations* of reason as suggested by Kant at the beginning of *Critique of Pure Reason*. Nothing obliges us to obey to any exclusivist deity, and nothing whatsoever obliges us to submit to necessity.

The most renowned attempt of insubordination to necessity is Plato's, whose philosophy nevertheless evaded reality and took refuge in fantasy. His was a failed insubordination dominated by (reversed) determinism, whereas the most prominent example of abnegation to necessity is Aristotle's, who invites us to halt before necessity. Both stances are metaphysical: the first assumes a substrate beneath necessity; the second reinforces a belief in facts. Neither spiritualism nor empiricism satisfies the passion of creative thought. Unless it is a materialist spiritualism, i.e. materialism open to the mystery of matter. We are indebted to Hume for his discovery that 'necessary' ties, normally attributed to phenomena, are connections between events and that one who speaks of necessity is like someone who dreams of being awake but, once awake, fails to perceive its reality. The Scottish philosopher did not go beyond that point yet succeeded in glimpsing the *possibility* of awakening. It is possible to wake up to necessity (according to Kierkegaard's and Shestov's encouragement), to *actively* accept it, breaking the spell of the millennial slumber of western thought. Probably the Greeks of the tragic and pre-Socratic era knew such awaken condition, but what we have inherited has been filtered through the Stoics. For Seneca not even the deity can afford the luxury of creation because it too obeys necessity. For Cicero fate guides the willing and drags the unwilling. At the opposite/complementary pole we find Plato, harbinger of any spiritualism to come, whose stance is characterized by the refusal of necessity and the emphasis on the visual faculty, on a cognitive intuition bestowed upon us by reason, whose supreme gift stages a curse: self-contentment, which slips into self-satisfaction.

What's more, Plato hesitates to surrender completely to a spiritual vision which might end up promoting evil and leading us away from philosophy, i.e. from the practice of death. Acquiring cognitive vision and cultivating intuition is therefore for Plato the practice of evil.

From Plato to Pascal to the XIV Dalai Lama our 'natural' human tendency is recognized as ascribing truth to pleasure, happiness and profit, whether personal or spiritual.

Every field of knowledge and inquiry is therefore passively subordinated to *Ananke*, goddess of necessity. There are a few exceptions here and there, mainly artists, poets, or poets/philosophers, thinkers who, like Kierkegaard, entrust themselves into the arms of the Absurd. They are poets in the wide sense: not mere purveyors of beautiful verse but individuals who actively accept tragic joy. They are *strong poets*, Rorty would say, individuals committed to aesthetics but not lulled by metaphysics, not hiding finitude within the sublime, or human imperfection at the core of any new interpretative system. Here perception of eternity takes place via the finitude of time: Proust's lesson, via Benjamin's interpretation and also Baudelaire's lesson of how small the world is under the gaze of memory. Neither eternalism, nor materialism; with her eyes wide open, the poet journeys through living-and-dying and learns her trade at the school of dying (*apothnêskein*); she familiarizes with the inexorable and delicate reality of death, our certain future. The poet becomes friend and accomplice of living-and-dying, accepts necessity with dignity. Her knowledge/wisdom ceases to be mere reshuffling of an ancient and venerable vocabulary and brings together *meditatio vitae* and *meditatio mortis*. One who willingly submits to such difficult and sublime apprenticeship no longer hunts for the essence but will express in every gesture the potency, vulnerability and paradox of being human, beyond good and evil, beyond pain and pleasure, including the pleasure of contemplation.

The realized Buddha retraces his steps and goes to the market place. He has nothing to teach: the ineffable remains ineffable, not subordinated to the useful, to mercenary virtue or to the fetishes of property, status, and knowledge.

Asleep, Dreaming of Being Awake

Moralists, scientists and priests braved necessity and necessity won. From each of these characters society receives information, useful to enable it to go on sleeping and, while asleep, dreaming to be awake. From radical methodologies of awakenings we learn how to sleep even deeper. Even the Buddha's teaching "Be an island onto yourself" is transformed into isolationism and pseudo-autonomy, in contentment and bourgeois refusal to measure oneself against alterity.

Every radical philosophy, initially conceived as exploration, ends up bolstering metaphysics and regales us with an edifying new system. Among nineteenth century philosophers Kierkegaard and Nietzsche made risky adventures out of philosophy and spirituality, recognizing faith as faith in the absurd. From the *knight of resignation* Kierkegaard moved to the *knight of faith*: not a crusader, but one who emerges from the ruins of history with a smile of joy for the plenitude of his experience and a smile of mockery towards history, the evil judge to whose deceptive sovereignty Hegel and the European bourgeoisie paid unprecedented homage.

Nothing is impossible for those who abandoned every hope and every creed, for those who abandoned their membership of the idolatrous factions of worldly or otherworldly salvation, for one who still has faith and remains serene and cheerful having experienced groundlessness and having gone beyond reason and knowledge.

From the apotheosis of doubt and resignation we move towards longing for the impossible; from tribal exile and psychic estrangement to the dignity of being *other*. That such a feat should take place via the route of exile and estrangement rather than via the hubris of scientism or religion reassures us against the danger of Titanism, the substitution of the deity with one's own ego. The empty sky takes the place of the deity, and the first messenger from this vertiginous place is the vivid, contingent and miraculous presence of the other. This presence is only acknowledged negatively in the Bible, in the systems of logic and dialectics – at the most as 'object of study'. Religion and science bow to necessity with prayers and mathematical formulae and both fail to recognize the other, unless it manifests as Messiah, or as realized being, or as a solid entity to be studied.

Mainstream western thought still depends on classic German philosophy, i.e. it is infatuated with all things mechanical. Even Hegel's 'Spirit' turns out to be nothing but that same Kantian practical reason thanks to which one behaves as if God existed, the soul were immortal and the will free. With alarming optimism, Kant goes as far as to affirm that there would be no human deed one could not predict in the chain of cause and effect. We find the same mechanical determinism in the law of *karma* and in fatalism. Precisely on the basis of such mechanical vision emerges the glorification of individual freedom, a veritable prisoner's day dream, the foreboding of truth among the inhabitants of Plato's cave and the first hint perhaps of the genuine awakening evoked by Plotinus. But dreaming of freedom does not set the prisoner free; instead, it confines him further in a cell on whose walls he has now etched clouds and sky.

The poet/philosopher cannot afford to comply with such tame fantasies: Orpheus does not fear his descent into Hades. Hamlet follows the counsel given by his father's ghost. Don Quixote creates a vibrant and heroic reality. Pygmalion demands the miracle. A youth gives his life for a night of love with Cleopatra. What if liberation resided *outside* the domains of practical reason and spirit? What if non-reactive activity belonged to an unlegislated domain? What if

Kant disobeyed the categorical imperative? What if Hegel violated Spirit?

The task of an individual is to abandon individualism; the task of every high civilization is to abandon a belief in its eternal endurance. Active acceptance of one's own finitude in an individual is not a sign of weakness but of strength. Equally, an understanding of its own inevitable demise is in a civilization a sign of greatness rather than failure. The instinct of self-preservation is characteristic of a sick organism and belongs, on a societal level, to the bourgeois spirit forever attempting to defeat impermanence through acquisition and expansion. On the other hand, a healthy organism can envision its own downfall.

The first tangible sign of the presence of death is the presence of the other, of the neighbour whose mystery I will never disclose and whose implicit demand forces me to give birth to myself. I no longer try to conquer death but instead try to be free of living-and-dying by fully participating in living-and-dying: realizing transcendence via a descent into immanence. I must then be able to admit that it is not within my power to observe the unfolding of living-and-dying from the outside or imagine the unborn and the undying as separate states. This admission of absence of an objective perspective is what I call integrity. Awakening takes place in the instant, in the heart of living-and-dying. Life does not hinder death and death does not hinder life.

In the same way we ought to resist the artifice of creating cosmologies and manufacturing brands of redemption: if there is salvation, it is an existential salvation, awakening to the emancipation of a will in harmony with becoming.

Wisdom spurs us not to linger on within *samsara*, whereas compassion invites us not to loiter in *nirvana*. The ethics emerging within the heart of samsara, in the miasma of a transitory life is another name for the *Dharma*, for the law of dependent origination (*paticcasamuppada*) whose handiwork cannot be understood through theories of immanence and transcendence. Far from being an abstract notion, dependent origination can be apprehended as *contingency*, as something, in Stephen Batchelor's words, "that depends on something else for its existence".[9]

Is it possible to create a cosmology of awakening readdressing the relationship between time and space? Compared to space, time is usually considered inner, owing to its bi-dimensional and dynamic structure. Kant understood time as inner intuition; Husserl saw the intentionality of consciousness; Heidegger founded his conception of Being-in-the-world in the concreteness of time. In all these examples, time has supremacy over space, something due to the predominance of the self as point of reference and reflection.

Reorganizing the correlation space/time by giving more emphasis to space would involve instead a de-centering of the self and an opening to the impact and reverberation brought about by the presence of the other. Predominance of space over time entails a re-evaluation of *experience* understood as *exteriority* rather than *Erfahrung*, which is effectively *surfing*, skipping on the multiple surfaces of sensory data without a transformative impact.

It is from space, from the vast experiential field that the individual emerges, and not the other way around. Experience is inclusive. In its search for a transcendental and universal principle, western metaphysics has neglected the experiential dimension. A conscious descent into the realm of experience opens us not to transcendence but, as we have seen, to a *trans-descent* – not the 'pure experience' longed for by some phenomenologists but a more concrete aim leading us to greater participation. From such voluntary descent into the experiential domain ethics is born, no longer dependent on the classic matrix subjectivity/objectivity; in trans-descent, things emerge and the self is forgotten (but not neglected) and what remains is the incessant activity of becoming. The ethics emerging from such an event is intuitive, and the response to alterity is originated by the impact alterity has on the subject: a manifold response of unpredictable and disconcerting beauty.

Saigyo, a twelfth-century Buddhist monk and poet, at the age of twenty-three renounced his position of court *samurai* and wandered through Japan. One day he happened to pass by a semi-abandoned temple. At the end of the main hall he saw an altar. He did not know what it represented yet found himself weeping.

Heteronomous and Autonomous Ethics

For heteronomous ethics, morality derives from external authority;

48

we obey orders from God and the sovereign. Apotheosis of this is Duns Scotus's stance: God does not command us to do certain things because they are good; rather, they are good because prescribed by God. For heteronomous ethics, human nature is essentially wicked – a point of view shared by Hobbes and by anyone who abandons the hard schooling of individuality in favour of obedience to the impersonal law: to do good in deference to the greatness of king, law or deity.

Autonomous ethics is complex and multi-faceted, and here I borrow Nishida's categorization[10] who subdivides it into rational, hedonic, and active ethics.

Rational Ethics

Rational ethics, based on the intellectual theory of ethics, sees good and evil according to the criteria of true and false. For the English rationalist theologian Samuel Clarke (1675–1729), relationships between things are as clear as mathematical principles – to obey God is to obey the highest rational principle. Will, feelings and instincts are not taken into consideration, an attitude which reminds one of the radical rationalism of the Stoics and the Cynics, where there is little room for human empathy.

Hedonic Ethics

Hedonic ethics, proposed by Aristippus and Epicurus, institutes the domain of an ethics of hygiene aimed at upholding egoic serenity, a perspective pre-dating the universalizing hedonism of utilitarians such as Jeremy Bentham. Even a conventional Kantian will oppose hedonism and utilitarianism because such positions fail to include the non-rationality of altruism. We love the other in spite of and at the expense of egoic calculation. Even the shadow of a recondite gain or pleasure would prevent the wanton joy of giving. The hypothetical Kantian thinker I have conjured up would place his value judgment in the heart of inner necessity, of 'inner' experience rather than the actualization of ideal values and principles.

Active Ethics

Active ethics has its foundations in Aristotle: life's aim would be *eudaimonia*, happiness, reductively understood, as we have seen, as triumph of reason rather than attention to the *daimon* and the *daimonic*. But even the Aristotelian version is in disagreement with uncritical submission to duty and the law, with the cheap moralizing normally peddled as ethics. Aristotelian *entelechy* includes both the manifest completeness of an entity and the potential achievement of such completeness. Given that what is manifest is in harmony with its potential, it acquires beauty, but this beauty is the illegitimate daughter of the goddess of reason. Not having gone through the upheavals of the daimonic, Aristotelian beauty must finally appeal, in order to preserve its Doric harmony, to law and duty – external and interiorized in the alleged self-sufficiency of an original and transcendental consciousness – a move not entirely dissimilar from Kant's and even Husserl's, which ends up re-affirming the transcendental reality of the self. This is of course a solemn affirmation – the pronouncement of a sublime self, able to do good, to perceive the essence of things through the power of intuition. It is the declaration of self heroically disentangled from sidetracking impulses and cravings, a spiritually greedy self who has not resisted the excesses of wisdom. In other words, this is the pronouncement of a self *not entirely human*. Witnessing in bewilderment the emergence of such a moral, spiritual and transcendental self, we awkwardly applaud the triumph of interiorized law and of the exclusivist God who establishes his violent rule in the psyche in the name of integration. The very idea of the self is modified: from a self at the mercy of its desires to a morally unsullied self. And yet what is lost is precisely the prized awareness of its organismic and provisional nature – a glimmer of humanity, possibly the only hope of deliverance.

Crystallization of the self through individuality is a necessary step – from egoist pleasure to a form of individualism able to include the ineffable: an event poetically illustrated in many traditions. In Zen, this is described as 'great death' or *kensho* – seeing into one's own nature.

His Majesty the Subject

Most of modern epistemology has restored the sovereignty of the subject, attributing to it characteristics once belonging to God alone. Transcendental idealism – from Kant to Husserl and to most positivist thought – sees the subject as creator and knowledge and understanding as acts of creation. Life and nature are perceived as chaos which must be brought to order by the intervention of humanity and culture. The next step sees the creation of a transcendental 'I' separate from its own existence, from the world and other beings. In transcendental philosophy as in positivism every form of relating is explained as the subject in relationship with plural objects.

Obedience to divine law and the *polis*, and the sovereignty of the transcendental 'I' both obscure the nature of ethics. Ethics must travel different paths that recognize the impermanent nature of the subject: these are paths of initiation because they require a necessary death and rebirth. They require the perception of emptiness and an adequate response to the ethical demand imposed by the presence of the other. In both cases we find ourselves outside the domain of law and duty.

Opus contra Naturam

If ethics belonged solely to the human domain, as neo-Darwinians such as Richard Dawkins believe, it would then be a sort of rebellion, the *opus contra naturam* of a species and, within the species, of unusual individuals who in given circumstances would respond ethically or heroically. The individual would become creator of an ethics *uprooted* from nature, a subject who alone opposes the tyranny of a selfish gene. For humans to enforce a moral law onto their own nature means that humans are an unfriendly lot and that ethics is there to varnish the savagery of *homo homini lupus*, a formula unfair to humans and wolves alike. To believe that human beings are radically different and separate from the animal kingdom – able to receive religious precepts (and from them derive *a priori* moral principles) is a form of anthropic negation, i.e. the refusal to accept the characteristics we humans share with animals, whereas postulating that nature and animal species are endowed with moral qualities presents us with the opposite problem of anthropocentrism.

The Ethical Demand

We experience mutual trust everyday, whether we meet friends, acquaintances or strangers. The trust we have in others does not conceal but increases the menace, or the evil that the other, according to Sartre, represents. Suspended in the uncertainty of the other's response, in relatively normal situations we opt for trust. This trust goes beyond good manners; it makes us vulnerable to the other, an act of surrender by which we often risk hurt and disappointment each time the gift of surrender is not reciprocated. Trust means faith in the continual renewal of life: we offer to others the freedom and opportunity to change, to be other and by doing so we affirm becoming. Trust is the refusal to reduce human nature to a gamut of reactive and static forces. It is a gift, to ourselves and others; the freedom to respond actively and with awareness with new expressions. Trust is not heroic but the simple basis of conversation.

We discover the very real impact we have on others, and such discovery contradicts the dominant vision of an encapsulated self, immune to external influences. We discover that we are an integral part of the world and destiny of others. This finding is unusual, not only because awareness of everyday occurrences is rare as most of us sleepwalk through existence, but also because we prefer to anesthetize the awareness that our words and deeds cause joy and pain to others as well as influence their choices in life. I become simultaneously conscious of my power and of my responsibility. The latter is a response to what the existential theologian Løgstrup calls the *ethical demand*, the silent request, implied yet imperious, coming forth from the other's presence even before moral and religious injunctions, even before a revelation or a conversion. Before the mind finds the time to manufacture a noumenon, the phenomenon itself demands my attention by summoning me to an adequate response. And it is by this response that I become for the first time human.

Because of its double nature of *risk* (opening to the other) and *response* (to the ethical demand), communication cannot take place between intact individuals but instead via a shared wound. The wound is original; it represents imperfection, finitude, and the inherent fragility of being human. Allowing the other to see me in my essential nakedness is precisely the prerequisite of communication. Thus understood, communication, premise and frame of ethics, is beyond the law. Social conventions may at the most *facilitate* relating between people, protecting us from psychic over-exposure, but they are not *ethical*. Good manners dictated by goodness and kindness do succeed in sustaining more or less stable affiliations. They do not respond to the silent ethical demand but primarily to the expectations and complex strategies of the self. Taking mutual pleasure in the placid ambience of anaemic, risk-free encounters, or wishing to change the other through moralistic judgement: both these modes of relating pervert communication. They might be useful in maintaining the status quo, in prolonging moribund institutions, but are useless to genuine communication.

Rejecting established norms presents us, however, with nearly insurmountable difficulties. Without resorting to some form of mediation, two people will find themselves fumbling in the waves of immediacy and passion. Non-mediated love easily becomes hatred, mutual consummation, irruption of chaos and absurdity. Staggering unexpectedly in a universe where nothing is certain, whose mechanism soon proves defective, most of us will flounder. Every *debâcle* is different: from estrangement to compulsive belonging, from isolation to conformity. Those who are able to resist the intensity brought about by lack of mediation without floundering find their way to a love devoid of sentimentality. The ethical demand does not require tearful exhibitionisms of the heart but a clear response and the ability to show one's nakedness and finitude to the other. However, absence of mediation quickly leads most people away from ecstatic union to desire to possess, to jealousy and isolation from the world. Here mediation is inevitable, the transformation of the event in necessity, through the creation of a *third*: an offspring, or a creative project of shared existence.

What happens when the absence of mediation overflows? The flame of love becomes anger. Yet, there is still hope, because anger is intensity and desire to right a real or imaginary wrong. But when the immediacy of love is transformed into the perverse intimacy of hatred, we admit our own inferiority towards the other. This is because we hate those towards whom we feel inferior. We hate those who would defeat us if we were to openly challenge them. *Hatred* (unlike anger, whose fire is pure) *is simulation.* We refuse to admit our helplessness and project our impotence on the other thus succeeding in maintaining some sort of intimacy with our opponent, in reversing ecstatic union into the perverse bond of hatred.

Mediation, granted by common interests, mitigates the intensity of the erotic-religious vision and introduces an intermediate realm. This is not necessarily translated into abdication to established tradition and its rules. In fact during the static phase following the *event*, a healthy distance from rules is concomitant to their observance. Without distancing ourselves from established rules, all we do is dogmatically adhering to them, a stance common to any fundamentalism, whether secular or religious. Ethics operates beyond and before the rules; it is born out of the aspiration to provide an adequate response to the silent demand of the person facing me – there is no time to consult a code of conduct before acting. We consult the code and appeal to morality in order to demonstrate our own superiority and gloat from the peak of our respectability.

An appeal to ethics is subversive in an era when the imperative of the super-ego has metamorphosed into the mantra *enjoy,* echoed by the multinational corporations who in selling us one of their numerous toys instruct us to smile happily while we perform the one deed on which western democracies place their faith: *shopping*, running around grasping whatever might fall from the plastic cornucopia of global capital. It is also true that ethics' subversive plea can turn into new forms of duty and guilt, or provide a frustrated individual with the compensatory makeshift of a utopian mission in which ethics itself becomes dogma: doing good for others becomes then an imposition, and loving kindness becomes spiritual arrogance, for I delude myself if I think I know what others need.

Every relationship is a power relationship, and ethics must take this realistically into account. The attempt to adequately respond to the ethical demand places us outside the sphere of good manners and the shared untruths implied by their implementation. It also places us outside the arrogance of wishing to change others by utilizing an ideological frame or a belief system. It is hard to come up with an adequate response; the other's demand is implicit, and its possible expression does not take place within stultified social norms. There is no indication; there is no map, and moral rules at the most approximate the response to the radical demand.

One-way Ticket

The flame of Eros does not guarantee *ethos* or love. Erotic passion leaves us partly immune to a deeper connection, in spite of the awe-inspiring intensity of the flame encircling us. In Løgstrup's definition, erotic passion is the meeting point of the *unknown* and the *uncommitted*. At the opposite pole we find the idealization of love and the denial of the erotic.

Consciousness is movement towards exteriority – it is a one-way ticket. A form of awareness originating within the subject and promptly returning to the subject (or awareness devoid of desire hence sheltered from the danger of a crisis which follows the unfolding of desire) does not deserve to be called consciousness.

The Chinese ideogram equivalent to the word *crisis* is made up of two elements, *danger* and *opportunity*. The shift towards exteriority leads us to innocence and the opportunity to cut through the alleged solidity of the self. It does not stage a homecoming but becomes dispersed in multiplicity. This is an act of desertion and renunciation: desertion of the empire of the self-same, renunciation of our anxiety to belong to a tribe huddled around its deity. It is an act of goodness, of *crazy* goodness, one that repudiates idolatry *tout court* but also the various idolatries whose revered mantras adorn the variegated layers of our primary illusion of identity: religion, nationality, soil, custom.

Some may rightly object that it was global capitalism that eroded local and diversified life, substituting it with a fluidity which is the fluidity of the market, with a false freedom dictated by profit and with an alienated universality. But the unmotivated goodness of ethics is at the opposite pole: it achieves universality by accident, through an act of generosity deliberately exposing me to excess, by inciting a crisis, inviting chance. I discover that only by meeting exteriority through desire and abandon, consciousness is born. The urgency of this shift dethrones death, if by death we mean nothing-ness and non-being, i.e. the notion of death the bourgeois borrowed from Cain, and which reduces others to objects in a transaction.

The shift towards exteriority walks the vertiginous space which separates me from death; it is the space of not-knowing – not of Socratic not-knowing, that juggler's trick in the circus of dialectics, but of not-knowing understood as intimate vertigo, a form of inti-macy which is hospitality and friendship rather than acquisition or even 'love'. If dialectical not-knowing belongs to dialogue, not-knowing-as-intimacy belongs instead to poetry and meditation, to the lovers' whispers and the faltering speech of the dying.

Not-knowing as intimacy comes *before* dialogue, in the same way as ethics comes before dialectical reason. If we accept this hypothesis, language is no longer the deity but becomes hospitality, a form of welcoming. In welcoming I renew my non-belonging to the soil; I confirm my fleeting nature, my non-substantiality; in welcoming I affirm my ability to receive, that is, my ability to learn. This is not an irrational stance, because it is reason that conceives a welcome, and in so doing contradicts maieutics and introduces *studium*, i.e. friend-ship, dedication to the good of others. *To study the self is to love the self*, that self that emerges for the first time in the encounter with the other, a self in which knowledge and wisdom are not innate, or in perpetual expectancy of a Socratic midwife or of the imaginary graft of Platonic memory. Learning is born out of the encounter with the existent. It is born in the heart of the dwelling – a transitory place, a confined, even secret garden, still a window nevertheless, framing the view of the horizon.

From our dwelling of dust and clay we experience the infinite sky. With embodiment the secular mystery of multiplicity is born, and finding ourselves swimming in it, no alterity is absolute alter-ity. In this I part ways with Levinas who saw alterity proper in the feminine. True, my own legitimate escape from the neuter solitude of being does take place in the dwelling via the encounter with a woman. Eros leads me out of the mesh of Platonism, manifesting as desire. And yet Eros does not lead me, as Levinas would have it, out-side phenomena, in an undefined elsewhere soon to be defined by the normalized yearnings of religion. It leads me, to be sure, to the presence of the other and outside Husserl's transcendental ego. Eros is reclaimed, stripped of Platonic and Christian garments, restored to the noise and dust of the street, to the precarious yet sovereign existence of a child beggar. Thus in receiving the guest, the host is himself received by his own dwelling. The owner is happily expropriated; emptied of ipseity, the subject becomes a tenant: hospitality precedes property.

We find ourselves in a different territory from the juridical and political sphere where peace treaties are stipulated in the brief interval between a bombardment and a genocide. Hospitality is the possibility of peace as suspension of the self, *epoché*, a radical stance which disintegrates the neutrality of Heidegger's being. Hospitality is not the Open (*Offenheit*), unless we apprehend it as vulnerability and not as in the two more common meanings of openness of an object to another object (the third analogy of experience in the *Critique of Pure Reason*), or as openness of a being thrown in the world. This stance re-instates subjectivity as hospitality rather than interiority.

Sacrifice

Is there room for sacrifice in ethics? Sacrifice is first of all renunciation of allegedly inexhaustible potentialities and the resulting realization that the choice awaiting me at each turning ends up shaping me. Sacrifice is also dedication to a cause, for instance to *justice*. This form of sacrifice has a sacred aura, akin to a message that reaches our living room from the trenches. Unlike subjective protest, sacrifice is an act of generosity courting universality and wrongly opposed to individuality. This is because we still apprehend the latter as solipsism and are ensnared between two equally totalizing, illusory polarities: neutral universality and individualist revolt. A way out of this impasse may be the notion of the *debt before the loan*, the strange freedom born out of a thorough assumption of responsibility. This stance – which could be defined as *phenomenology of hospitality* – still accepts the axiom of interdependence yet deliberately lingers on what has been neglected by dialogical and inter-subjectivist orthodoxy, namely separation. *Ethics* is a Greek approximation of the Hebrew *kadosh*, i.e. the sacredness of what is separate. To be able to utter a sincere *yes* in the midst of impermanence: in this consists my adherence to the sacred. I say *yes* with trepidation, for it requires suspension of the self and a withdrawal. Withdrawing opens a gap in time itself, creates a dislocation which perturbs the linearity of time, in the way a surprise or even unwanted visit does, or a meeting with the stranger and the foreign.

As a vestige of God himself (*Exodus*, 33), revelation is visitation, an unexpected call, an accident which is opportunity and risk, a crisis denting my habitual representations. There is no initiation proper for those unable to receive others in the dwelling of their subjectivity. There is no rebirth for those who evade an encounter with the foreign. There is no ordination, for this is not ritualistic obedience to liturgy but pursuing a discipline of affirmation. There is no *res publica* without libations offered to the goddess of hospitality, without intolerance making room for unmotivated love. Hospitality makes us human, not because it harmonizes us to an hypothetical basic goodness dormant at the heart of our being, but because to become human implies an irreverent challenge to the Platonic *polemos*, to the Kantian state of war (*Zustand des Krieges*) and threat (*Bedzohung*), to Hobbesian cynicism and Hegelian dialectics.

Whether peace is a natural state or not is an ontological question to which ethics refuses to respond, or to which it responds through unconditional, extra-juridical hospitality, where peace precedes the very idea of nature. The so-called hospitality offered by nation-states is, on the other hand, conditional, hypocritical, utilitarian, for it reflects market fluctuations and international diplomatic relations. The peace brought forward by ethics is instead anarchic, born out of the suspension of the *arché* when faced with the vivid presence – sacred because separate – of the other. It is, perhaps paradoxically, by inhabiting this position that we simultaneously build our dwelling – no longer conceived as an area circumscribed by a wall or a fence but as sojourn, as a space nurturing the distance and separation of desire. The dwelling ceases to be the soil on which I plant the flag of a particular imagined community, spurred on by the arbitrary blessings of the state and the deity superseding it. It becomes instead temporary shelter from the vicissitudes of contingency, a place where I can welcome exteriority and begin an education.

I realize that such an anarchic stance risks turning into the egotism of subjectivity, the conservative protest of the individual who opposes the state and ends up worshipping herself. In order to avoid this slip, Levinas proposes the image of paternal fecundity, a sort of primordial hospitality which evades both individualism and the universalizing tyranny of the state. The Levinasian move reminds one obliquely of Lacan, for whom the law of desire can unfold solely under the aegis of a structuring super-ego. We are reminded that before we think of self-preservation we must take care of the widow, the orphan, and the foreigner.

I is Another

The notion of ego identity has never been entirely convincing and from the impossibility of demonstrating ipseity Marx derived the fertile notion of *alienation*. A few decades later, with the October revolution curdling into Stalinism, European thought re-formulated the notion of alienation within metaphysical, rather than social terms. Disconnected from society and history, Lukács's *alienation* became Heidegger's *falling*. Lukács's unacknowledged influence on Heidegger is now documented as the latter's distortion of a notion originally rooted in the colonization and manipulation of the everyday.

Heidegger also intervened to salvage subjectivity by linking Husserl's transcendental ego to the edifice of metaphysics, reclaiming the subject as receptacle of the neutral glow of being. Yet being, Levinas reminds us, needs humanity as nature needs the soil. The neutrality of being represses and annihilates the singularity of the person; the paradox is that for Heidegger it is eventually the elected individual who becomes messenger and poet of being. This was effectively a regression, after a long detour, to the metaphysics of the subject; it was the implosion of the very notion of *Being-in-the-world*, a potential alternative to both the Cartesian self and the Freudian psyche.

A vision of a subjectivity unencumbered by universalism and solipsism is inevitably associated with vulnerability. It may be useful to ask, alongside Levinas, whether Rimbaud's *"Je est un autre"* might be interpreted in more than one way: alongside the classic interpretations of the *I* as primary alienation and of the primordial impossibility for the self to know itself, it might also be read as *accusing oneself* in the presence of another person's suffering. This would confirm the thesis that *what is human is exterior*, unfolding in the open, exposed to the elements and the vicissitudes of nature and culture. One might also ask whether identity itself is multiple, problematic, and continuously subject to change. Subjectivity is incapable of closing in on itself; the senses are naturally linked to exteriority which is much more than a bundle of stimuli or a cause producing an effect.

The other for whom I suffer summons me to existence, resuscitates me from my abode, and incites me to realize my paradoxical subjectivity. The other uncovers me, and in her presence I surrender. I had longed for her apparition; her visitation confirms my subjectivity as *being-for-the-other*.

Journey to a Foreign Land

During the shipwreck of being I am summoned and while I hurry to the meeting place I gather my thoughts. I catch myself thinking – before logic, before conceptualization, even before the unwanted gift of a transcendental self.

In the enigma of my subjectivity, I am being thought. Thought befalls me so that I, simulacrum of the true person of no status, may appear before the other and offer my *potlatch*, the use-less, i.e. sacred, expenditure of my life. No fanfare celebrates the emergence of such individuality; no triumphal little march, whether nuptial or funereal; no bucolic sonnet to friendship or love. Instead, the body exposed to weather and caress, to encomium and shame for this birth too is pain.

Philosophy is, like death, a journey to a foreign land (Plato, *Phaedrus*, 61). Unless it is tourism, travelling means experiencing. What is experience? For Levinas, something deserves the name 'experience' if it leads me outside so-called interiority, outside what I consider to be my nature. Truth implies experience, the opening up of assumed interiority. Philosophy is then *heteronomy*, i.e. enquiry into exteriority.

A more conventional view sees philosophy as free investigation of a subject who, after excursions in unknown lands, comes back to itself, identical to itself. This view presupposes the autonomy of the subject and reduces the other to the self-same. This mode of thought has provided conceptual ornament to Empire, colonialism and the exporting of identity and 'our way of life'. It is the very opposite of religiosity (understood as revelation of a deity whose presence is radically other) and of transcendence (as revelation of what is extraneous, whether religious or not).

Mainstream philosophy is therefore a form of autarchy or *egology*, and a psychology replicating its themes and motifs would not engender psycho-therapy but rather ego-therapy. The error in this mode of doing psychology consists in confusing the otherness of psyche – its vastness and inexplicability – with the atomized intimacy of personality or with an autonomous and mechanical psychic apparatus. Even the relationship with the *object*, as rendered by the Kleinian tradition, avoids otherness because the existence of an object presupposes the *a priori* existence of a network of relationships, of a net of interdependence which bypasses inalienable separation.

Through cognition the individual is grasped and apprehended, becoming a sample to be examined in the science lab. The symbolic translation of such a philosophical move is *money*, which allows us to momentarily *possess exteriority* by destroying both its autonomy and our chance to learn. In the world we have constructed, freedom manifests as wealth, and reason is subjugated around the clock to the god of money, elaborating for us strategies of power and appropriation.

Of Conscience as Bad Conscience

The revelation/apparition of the other on the horizon of my consciousness carries a fundamental message: *do not hurt me.* The injunction derives from the asymmetric encounter with the other rather than from divine command. The other's nakedness, the vulnerability of his being, those eyes looking at me – if I am able to listen, all this brings to an end the melodrama of my isolation. When isolation ends, individuality is born. Response to otherness is therefore neither duty, divine or moral injunction nor the aspiration, dictated by the super-ego, of being righteous when relating to others. If I forget that the other is also potentially evil; if I forget that the other is also *the thing*, monstrous and oppressive, I may easily slip into idealizing the other, a stance to which Levinas has not been immune. What remains valid and genuinely radical in Levinasian thought is the anarchic aspiration to resist the ineluctability of domination as well as an ethical resistance to the imperialism of the self-same. That we may treasure such insights without having to package them as a new ideology is the task of anyone attempting to articulate the discipline of radical ethics. To this purpose the Nietzschean solvent may be useful – in the same way Nietzsche used the Heraclitean solvent – in order to suspend the periodic stagnation of ethics into a moral system. I refer the reader to the second book of *Genealogy of Morals*, particularly those paragraphs, from the fifteenth onwards, where Nietzsche questions the origins of bad conscience and finds a link in what he calls *instinct of freedom* (which he will later define as *will to power*).

> "This *instinct of freedom* made latent through force – as we have already understood – this instinct of freedom, forced back, trodden down, incarcerated within and ultimately still venting and discharging itself only upon itself: such is *bad conscience* at its origin, that and nothing more."[11]

In Nietzsche's *caveat* we perceive the healthy egoism of the artist who must counterweight the guilt which hampers the proudest instincts and curbs them into philistine goodness, suppressing the will to create. The super-ego in its crudest traits often lies in wait for those who venture along the route of ethical practice. Guilt and bad conscience are at the heart of the prohibition, both shadows of cultural conditioning.

Injunctions, traditionally handed down by patriarchy, increasingly originate in contemporary western societies within that intricate net of Christian and pseudo-socialist opinions universally known as *political correctness*, an expediently Apollonian way in which current bourgeois ideology has contained the unruly forces wrestling for social, racial and gender equality. At the front line of this veritable counter-reformation we find, sadly, mainstream psychotherapy, which having summarily given up its original transformative valence, is increasingly becoming re-education in social conformity.

At the heart of the psychotherapeutic enterprise we must instead place sublimation, understood as respect of the sublime longing of the subject and channelled into the rebuilding of lived narratives and into art. Gone the ancient link between subject and sovereign good, the difficult task of actualization is perhaps not given to all, with the exception perhaps of tragic natures able to host Dionysian joy. Most of us, confronted with the flames of the ethical demand, necessitate the symbolic and aesthetic protection offered by psychotherapy and art. Levinas seems to ignore the fact that two millennia of Judaeo-Christian ideology have flooded us with guilt and bad conscience, so that, when faced with the cutting blade of alterity, most of us will be unceremoniously vivisected.

Yet an adequate response is crucial if we wish to go on considering ourselves human, a response able to honour the ethical demand without running for cover under the abstraction of being or the consolations of bourgeois morality. Sublimation in all its forms offers such response,[12] and the acceptance of what Simon Critchley aptly calls "original inauthenticity", i.e. what resides at the heart of subjective experience in relation to an ethical demand which we do not fully understand and towards which we feel inadequate.[13] Humbly accepting our own limitations grants us a welcome respite from the super-ego's endless list of obligations.

For Plessner[14], human beings find themselves in an *eccentric* position. We do not coincide with ourselves but inhabit a gap between a physical and a psychological dimension. Embedded in the animal kingdom, we have deliberately placed ourselves outside it via an act of *Abgehobenheit*, or apartness.[15] In this peculiarly human situation of "mediated immediacy", the human being experiences herself *as* and *within* a thing, a thing differentiating itself from all other things because she is herself that thing. She finds herself sustained and surrounded by something that keeps resisting her. To fully recognize this condition liberates us from the obligation to tag along the latest epistemologies and invites us to accept the ambivalence between presence and apartness, proximity and remoteness, objectivity and subjectivity.

Critchley develops this notion in an interesting way, even though he risks constructing a sort of upside-down ontology – by extolling for example the virtues of *humour* in a very serious style. His conclusions are more convincing when he suggests how humour can become one of the less hostile functions of the super-ego.

Nothing to do With Love

It is a common misconception to confuse ethics with love, affectivity and subjective feelings. Alterity exists beyond my thirst; my desire is never satisfied. The other is inalienably separate, elusive, and unfathomable: through desire I am forced to lean over my isolation; this is how I learn and experience. Unsatisfied desire realizes itself as objectless desire, i.e. sacred longing outside the domain of convenience. The joy of Eros is born out of its absolute poverty, out of the solicitude and readiness to give oneself completely and receive nothing in return apart from a further widening of the abyss separating me from the other.

What is given is conferred as gratuitous expenditure – life itself is given to us for a brief time on the Earth's dreamy crust. The ethical response is giving away what time and space is presented to us. It is a way of dwelling on this Earth, nurtured by infinity and preceding the notion of individual freedom. Infinity frees us from the need to possess and presents us with a real alternative (even if only as an aspiration whose trajectory is being sketched for us) to the established curriculum of violence.

Encounter cannot take place via *techniques*. Only when techniques fail encounter becomes possible. Only by encountering alterity can *the present moment* occur, the *instant* rather than the customary verdict shutting out a past and prefiguring a future. We cannot of course inhabit pure encounter with otherness; its lyrical intensity would kill us if extended beyond those fortunate moments. But without it our existence is not living but surviving. Radical ethics abolishes the machinations of religious dogma and scientism and introduces in their place *absolute heterogeneity* which values difference and renounces both unity and universality by affirming separation and exile.

In *Saint Genet*, Sartre writes of *double exile*: exile from being and from having. He ascribes to Genet what Rougemont had ascribed to Don Juan when he said: "He *is* not enough to have and he does not *have* enough to be". The individual who accepts absolute heterogeneity comes to know the horror of solitude but also immortal enchantment, as Genet says through his character Querelle. He walks alongside an abyss, contemplating death, a truth denied by the *museums of living* of which we are the curators.

The ethical individual refrains from perpetuating the automatism of goodness as well as the officious banality of evil. She regains what is poetic in evil itself, uncovering a path leading to poetry and revolt. Without travelling on this path of desertion and disorientation, we remain forever inhibited, enmeshed within a Manichean honesty, able to empathize with the orphan but distancing ourselves from thieves and criminals. Without a rejection of the canons of morality and religion, ethics would be snugly absorbed by bourgeois liberalism and the injunctions of an atavistic super-ego. Without such revolt we cannot understand Genet's notion of *dignity*, i.e. the refusal of the exiled, the migrant and the oppressed to apply for membership of the herd which hosts him. There is a parallel here with the radical passivity expounded in Dharma teachings, for these encourage us to reject the seductions of identity, power and wealth and question the ethos of societies founded on greed and delusion.

For Sartre the dignity of the oppressed is *strategic* and will turn to revolutionary action once circumstances allow. But what is being questioned here is the very notion of dignity associated with the rank and authority of public office. Giorgio Agamben traces the creation of a 'theory of dignity' back to the jurists and canonists of the Middle Ages, explaining how in imperial Rome, as in monarchic France, this designated a fictitious entity, a sort of mystical body alongside the real body, and how this became, through morality, altogether separate from public office. The subsequent shift of the notion of dignity needs to be from morality to radical ethics, from the alleged autonomy of inner experience to deliberate leaning over towards alterity.

II

A HUMAN REVOLUTION

Ethical Life begins with Aesthetics

Aesthetics is an act of derealization of the real. It is the midwife of *justice* and *loyalty*. Justice is the most valid objection to the natural exaggerations of an individual who believes himself noble and virtuous, while loyalty is the solidarity limiting the insatiability of desire. Far from being ornamental, the aesthetic domain is crucial in giving expression to human experience and in attempting to de-colonize the everyday from the aims of the ego, of capital, and of religious mystification. There are striking similarities between the project of 'aesthetic revolution' (which began with Schiller's *Letters on the Aesthetic Education of Mankind* and continued in 1790 with the document known as the *Oldest System-Programme of German Idealism* attributed to Hegel, Hölderlin and Schelling) and Marx's writing of the 1840s. In these he writes of a *human revolution*, one that would abolish philosophy by consuming it (by bringing it to completion); a revolution close to the aesthetic paradigm, which would later create the foundation for an alliance, especially in the 1920s, between the artistic avant-garde and Marxist thinkers.

A human revolution is an aesthetic revolution, no longer dependent upon the categories of totality or limited within the stale opposition between the state and the wide community, but based instead on poetic education and on the principles of non-territoriality and solidarity with the dispossessed. If born out of an authentically ethical stance rather than dictated by natural social norms, justice and loyalty escape the compulsion of tribal belonging behind which hide totalitarianism and capitalist false democracy. It is in this context that must be understood, as we shall see, Genet's appeal in favour of betrayal as a way to preserve individual dignity.

In the oscillation between love and death, allowing the continuous sublime unfolding of becoming, death has the last word. Ethics and artistic creation juxtapose love and death in a non-competitive encounter. For the ancient Greeks, love is equal in strength to death (*krataia hōs thanatos agapē*); and for the Zen tradition living-and-dying (*shoji*) is one and the same.

Postcard with Camel

It is the norm for colonizers and settlers to denigrate indigenous populations. With an arrogance borrowed from philologists and philosophers, from those who relied solely on the reading of texts in building a world view, they have systematically destroyed (educated, civilized) indigenous culture. In Zionist documentaries of the 1930s, the territory is represented as unexplored, an empty space sporadically crossed by a picturesque Arab on a camel, adding an exotic note to the landscape. Reality appears fleetingly, obliterated by the usurper who likes to imagine that his invasion is an act of charity and of reclamation of the soil. As with the pioneers in America, obliteration of a society counts very little compared to the imperative of conquest and pillage. In both the examples of Israel and America usurpers were inspired by the Bible, by the spirit of aggression and the inflexible conviction to be in the right.

Of the Dignity of Betrayal

Patriotism is affirmation of an imaginary superiority, badly concealing a sense of inferiority. In the example of the Palestinian struggle, patriotism is instead a mirage, representing all that Palestinians never had: passport, territory, and a nation. The refugee similarly dreams of his homeland or of the future foreign land which will host him. The homeland demands that the individual respects rituals and formalities of tribal belonging in exchange for the expansion of one's ego into the ego of the nation, and this is why betrayal becomes an act of emancipation, proclaiming the freedom of the individual and the refusal to submit to the customs and rites of a specific group.

Betrayal exherts a greater fascination than loyalty, a fact that might be linked to its "forbidden vitality", as well as to the fact that it is an "uncanny form of intimacy".[1] Betrayal has its own scale of ethical values: E. M. Forster hoped he could bring himself to betray his country rather than his friend. A true rebel betrays history but is loyal to becoming. The only belonging possible to the rebel is alongside the oppressed – an ephemeral form of belonging, to be sure, lasting only as long as the revolt lasts, and ceasing to exist as soon as the refugee finds his elective land, the proletarian establishes his dictatorship, and the migrant finds himself integrated, having imbibed language and prejudices of the new land. For Genet the Palestinian uprising was not desire for a territory but an aspiration to dissolve the twenty two Arab nations and "garland everyone with smiles", creating in the process a hybrid yet fertile blending of Marxism with Islam.

A Revolution Against Being

We are passengers, constantly on the verge of leaving; soon we will be like ghosts, silhouettes from the past. Detained by the certain prospect of our own disappearance, we are linked to pure exteriority, our true place of birth, circumscribed by the walls of a dwelling made of stone and clay, of faiths and rituals. We must refute humanism, the subjectivism of the inner life, the cult of the human species, this titanic originator of laws and the artifices of art and science, unless it is a form of humanism capable of addressing the vulnerability and uncertainty of our condition and refusing customary plans of conquest and gratification. This same refusal inspired the Paris Commune, the upheavals of May 1968 in Europe and those of 1999 in Seattle, the Arab Spring and the *Occupy* movement, and indeed any event which will continue to open a breach in history and allow a glimpse of becoming.

The nature of these movements is anti-heroic, anti-capitalist, and anti-subjectivist, if we understand 'subject' as the bourgeois dummy that piles up merits, trophies and competences at the altar of ontology. The philosophical counterpart is a revolution against being and the very notion of being as well as the regional ontologies subcontracting their disparate identities, each of them founded on prevarication and violence. It is a genuine shift, leading us away from our perpetual fumbling in search of God's shadows and cut-rate essences. It is a shift that might introduce again the prophetic word: there is no I nor God if not in syntax; there is no being behind the curtain of becoming. This shift is not gratuitous: the sincerity of revolt – eternally betrayed, eternally elusive – is our only hope. It is an anarchic shift which, following Levinas's footprints, clumsily steals from Kant's architectural design and deliberately betrays its idealism. It is an anarchic shift stealing the radicalism of encounter from Levinas, yet discarding his Talmudic orthodoxy because this fails to recognize otherness in the Palestinians.

To the empire of the self-same, founded on possession and fear of otherness, European existentialism opposed a radical rationality, in the hope that it might help the individual discern the inevitability of anguish when faced with the non-substantiality of the self. Existentialism identified in *terror* the implicit motivation prompting the subject to a de-humanizing appropriation. Such a liberating discovery was hijacked by Heidegger's neo-idealism that re-introduced the idea of being and freedom of the subject who draws his *raison d'être* from abstract being. Heideggerian being is not *a* being but a *neuter* which organizes beings and to which one must sacrifice one's ethical response to otherness. That Heidegger succeeded in representing classic idealism under the guise of phenomenology is evidence of his philosophical genius. It also shows the ongoing difficulty European thought has in maintaining loyalty towards becoming.

In the name of being wars broke out and tyrannies came to be in defense of the undisputed and violent fetishes of property and exploitation. The history of being coincides with the history of western civilization and its gory patrimony. Yet within western civilization an *anti-tradition* also found expression, often emerging in the very heart of mainstream thought. Even in Plato, founder of that idealism which often denigrated lived life, we find an affirmation that places the Good above Being (*The Republic*, 517b, 518d). Even in

Descartes we find an analysis of infinity, inviting the subject to think beyond thought. Even though the Platonic Good is modelled on an idea external to phenomena, being is momentarily replaced by the Good. Even though Cartesian infinity is far from denting the rationalist edifice, the *cogito* opens to infinity. Are the notions of the good and infinity *a priori* ideas? Or are they rather *experiences*? We are challenged by infinity and otherness; when thinking infinity, thought extends beyond me. Its origin is not to be found in the inner life of the thinking subject, but, as we have seen, in desire. By approximating an adequate answer, desire becomes goodness, albeit a *crazy* sort of goodness for it goes against any project of acquisition and accumulation. It is a gratuitous hence sacred response, utilizing the surplus, i.e. the thought of infinity and encounter with otherness.

Levinas critiqued the inter-subjectivity found in three philosophers, Hegel (master/servant dialectics), Husserl (dependence of ego from alter ego) and Heidegger (for whom *Dasein* equals *Mitsein*), and in each of them found a misleading notion of symmetry which bypasses the fundamental traumatism of the subject and the asymmetry of every encounter. Yet Levinas's thought has been in turn subject to misinterpretation. The poetry of otherness found in Levinas engendered a vast literature of sentimental altruism, particularly in the field of psychotherapy, something that has made this difficult thinker more accessible whilst dampening the anarchic valence and the traumatic element present in encounter. The ethical Levinasian subject is not necessarily the *bodhisattva* of Buddhist lore, but a "traumatized neurotic", to borrow Critchley's expression.[2] Besides, there are instances where the moral ideal of the bodhisattva degenerates from empathic solidarity and courageous acceptance of samsara as nirvana into masochistic pietism.

Both the Levinasian and the Buddhist ethical subject belong to the *symbolic* domain, and their call must be answered symbolically rather than literally. A symbolic response will be ethical *and* political rather than hazily altruistic or geared towards the cultivation of an ornamental virtue and a positive karma accumulated with interests and dividends.

It is dangerous to respond *literally* to the Levinasian or the Buddhist imperative. The noble ethics of the sovereign good belongs to antiquity, to the Aristotles and the Aquinas, and is no longer accessible to us. We live in an alienated reality where relations among individuals are contaminated by profit and the false inter-dependence of cybernetics: given these conditions, what ethical redemption is possible, what happiness?

Buddhism and the new spirituality nowadays popular in the United States and in some parts of Europe propose again the opium of exotic happiness, surrogates to both the more dignified tragic-heroic condition implicit in the existentialist position and to the navigable alternative provided by artistic sublimation. Together with mainstream psychotherapeutic orientations and *new age* spirituality, institutionalized Buddhism flaunts the mirage of a wholesome normality which would give back strength to the exhausted and de-motivated individuals of the global village.

The project of radical ethics is placed at the opposite end, as aesthetic response aimed at rebalancing injustice and canalizing the infinity of desire. Animated by beauty and justice, transgressing the laws of utilitarianism, ethics answers to the excess of beauty by refusing to implode into the guilt and the pietism of ventures that approximate it but whose ethos they have usurped. The exigency posed by otherness is immediate, potent, and inhexhaustible: I must be able to answer it without being crushed or abdicating to a new metaphysics. Useful tools are phenomenology, art, anarchic non-violent revolt, and above all the creation of a new subjectivity capable of injecting poetry into the prose of the world. The ethics presented here is in many ways antithetic to Hegelism, not to the historicist, early Hegel to whom we owe the sophisticated antidote to eternalism, but to Hegelism understood as messianic doctrine of History and glorification of the state.

In the Marxist notion of alienation, and in the possibility of emancipation through a vision of a total human being, we recognize an endeavour in agreement with anarchist ethics. Like radical ethics, Marxism moves away from the ideal of a bourgeois humanity. The bourgeois believes he knows his identity. Such identity is illusory and founded on his possessions and commodities. If such identity deteriorates, anguish and unhappy consciousness will follow; an abyss opens between self and other – not the distance of otherness, but the distance between two *objects*. Here alienation is not only economic but tragically reflects the inability to consider the other: the life of the bourgeois is not only *fragmented* but also *artificial*, and this artificiality makes mystification possible.

The everyday is trivialized, made one with the world of commodities and profit, becoming dismal and mechanical repetition. As we have seen, the everyday in modern society is trivial not because inauthentic, i.e. removed from being, but because colonized by capitalism.

An opening into authenticity is possible, not via a passive contemplation of being but via art and a social engagement motivated by justice and solidarity – in other words via a move from *ontology* to *historicity*. Ethics goes beyond metaphysics: for instance, it recognizes the existential aspect of the expulsion from Eden, an event which becomes real and historical, manifesting as alienation. It is through alienation that the fullness of life is lost in the name of profit and of the spectacularization of existence. With this fall, life ceases to be lived experience and becomes 'culture' controlled by the experts. Reappropriation of the everyday means discovering the unknowability of what is familiar, for familiarity hides others. The exploration of the mysterious territory of the everyday, unknown and ambiguous, happens through art – theatre, poetry, the novel – and through radical ethics.

Liberation from alienation and the colonization of the everyday is possible; it is an epic undertaking, epic in the Brechtian sense, since it requires resolute decisions and the ability to see through a dense net of false needs. This is a quality belonging to discerning wisdom, able to perceive the suffering inherent in alienation and gradually foreshadowing a way out. The tools for this potentially liberating shift are meditation and art, which transform relaxation and free time from passive distraction (emptying existence of its contents) and ornament (concealing alienation with the cosmetics of fake reality) to the active cultivation of critical and playful faculties.

Because alienation invades not only work but also our so-called free time, it is from the latter that a dismantling of alienation can begin. History teaches, however, how the search for beauty and wonder did not engender liberation but the selling out of art, as happened with the debasement of Romanticism into Gothic and with the pseudo-ethics of moralist art. The god of money, prime maker and chief sorcerer of the west, dominates the proceedings.

A truly *affirmative art* does not denigrate the world but rehabilitates the everyday, freeing it from the clutches of capital, exalting its unfathomable nature. Affirmative art cannot but belong to the cultural patrimony of the Left, inasmuch as it is a form of critique inspired by justice and equality, unlike a metaphysical or mystical critique which inevitably ends up denigrating the everyday and assert ideals of perfection.

A human science will be able to articulate a creative understanding of the everyday, of what idealist philosophy rejects as ontic. In the heart of the humanities, whether psychology, psychotherapy, art or meditation, we find a vibrant interest in the everyday. Where else should we find the meaning of life if not in life itself? This commitment to the study and love of the everyday makes us painfully aware of the mystification it is subjected to by a dominant culture bent on eternalizing its own creed in order to maintain its privileges, in giving up individuality for individualism, in forfeiting common sense for *private logic*[3] hence to a private or deprived life, to the sadness of bourgeois existence, where each atomized being thinks itself unique.

In counteracting this downward movement, we effectively contribute to the creation of what Stephen Batchelor perceptively calls a *culture of awakening,*[4] an all-round, concerted effort aimed at demystifying and un-privatizing human existence, at making it pliable to creativity, enquiry, and wisdom. Art and psychology, love and meditation thus conceived open up a horizon beyond the fetishism of money and property. Devaluing money implies appreciating *wealth* which is, like power, a necessary instrument of emancipation. This is not a eulogy of poverty but the recognition of the real suffering of the have-nots, the unemployed, and the homeless who experience throwness and uncertainty in a tangible way.

In Marx we find a fertile relation between person and object well beyond ownership. The crucial element in Marx's critique of fetishism is that it is important not only to possess an object, but also to enjoy it, in the human and spiritual sense of the word, and in such enjoyment enter into relation with other beings. It is not so important that I possess a plot of land but that between me and the soil there is a reciprocity which in turn brings me close to others. In such a net of complex relations individuality is re-discovered as an integral and dis-alienated part of interdependence, which effectively constitutes a move from bourgeois individualism to free individuality. For this to occur it is necessary that money, essence of the alienated human being, be substituted by wealth.

It is difficult not to see the everyday as the domain of the non-philosophical or the raw material from where art and thought are extracted. It is difficult not to romanticize the everyday as the realm of the 'ten thousand things'. Culture and civilization blend in the everyday and emerge from it. Observing with equanimity the world of which we are part and remaining loyal to experience were the aspirations, only partially realized, of existentialism. We are indebted to existentialism and Marxism for the attempt to refrain from representing the everyday as inferior to the intellectual or spiritual domains and in this way avoid its diminution to a mere object of observation.

Technology of Mis-information

The other is at the same time alienation and freedom from alienation. Ethics takes into account conditioned reality yet responds to the other directly, taking into account the fundamental asymmetry of the I–Thou encounter. If we fail to understand asymmetry, we end up idealizing the encounter with the other and reinstating the evangelical ideology of a 'love' incapable of appreciating the very real burden of injustice. The function of social hierarchy is to obscure the gaps between social strata. The proliferation of images and information data dished out daily by modern technology, as the widespread manipulation of consensus masquerading as journalism mystify rather than clarify social reality. Un-weaving the thread of the social unconscious implies shedding light on the relations of economic production: knowledge forfeits the fatuity of classic epistemology and becomes active social critique and ethical action. To what purpose? Not in order to claim a slice of the cake at the banquet of the elite, but in order to undermine the very foundations of a socio-political reality that has elevated greed, ignorance and aggression to metaphysical heights. At what level? At the level of the everyday, i.e. of a province that since the demise of empire has been capitalism's new colony. The colonization of the everyday does not only concern the social sphere but goes right inside the psyche. The advent of the society of the spectacle and its acceleration via the technology of mis-information has reduced our capacity to cultivate imagination and to elaborate psychic forms and meanings. It has substituted the patient work of art and psychotherapy with a fetishism of the image, and direct encounter with digital solipsism.

Psyche is understood here in the Heraclitean sense, synonym of the vastness of phenomena, both internal and external. There is no contradiction between affirming psyche and being in agreement with the historicist project that denies essence to human nature and recognizes contingency. Historicism makes us aware of the transient nature of human values and helps us escape the priestly entanglements of dogmatic religion and scientism. It spurs us on to continue our investigation beyond the dogma of the former and the alleged objectivity of the latter.

In accord with the best phenomenological tradition, we can consider religious axioms and scientific formulas as *descriptions* to be pondered and considered alongside novels, chronicles, cartoons, plays and movies, and free ourselves from the yoke of imposed objectivity. Rather than giving in to the vision of convergence towards truth, we could celebrate and enjoy the proliferation of ideas and cultural/political movements inspired by the principles of justice and solidarity. The merit of these movements is having a vision of human potentialities, not in the name of a natural essence positioned underneath social conditionings but as an experiment in alteration of language and perception, as creation of conditions as yet barely glimpsed. This is of course poetic work, the work of a strong poet, of one who renews things by renewing the vocabulary, who gradually introduces a new language thus creating new ways of perceiving life and the world.

Changing the way in which we describe the world means changing who we are: a process that abolishes the arbitrary distinction between reality and appearance, the sublime and the everyday, the absolute and the relative. This distinction constitutes the main inheritance of mainstream philosophy; once this falls away, we are free to compare languages and descriptive modalities, to find new combinations and abandon the tyranny of traditions, of received and

76

obsolete wisdom, the tyranny of the past and solid entities which tradition imagines exist behind the curtain of language. Abandoning the aforementioned idolatries means questioning more effectively the revelations of all religious traditions and the presumptions of scientism.

The refusal to venerate an imaginary foundation of being opens up the possibility of greater freedom: there is no metaphysical basis to the teachings of the Buddha, but *dependent origination*, a fluid terrain similar to Heraclitus' *river*. That there is nothing beyond contingency is also the hypothesis of historicism from Hegel onwards, something which has found a creative interpretation in Rorty.

The Curse of Cain

At the origins of identity we find violence, the distinction between self and non-self, between *us* and *them*. Fear and hatred of the stranger is implicit in the Aristotelian principle of non-contradiction according to which A, in order to be A, cannot be B. Plato then prosaically reduced the subtlety of Heraclitean *polemos* to war against the enemy, the different, the foreign. But it is with the Bible that we have a consecration of the link between identity and violence. What defines Israel? Israel is the non-Egypt. Why violence? Because the Hebrew Bible is governed by the idea of *scarcity*, key principle in the genesis of identity. Violence is historically born with identity, and Cain's first act of violence is the demarcation of a border, the imaginary line traced between us and them.

The Hebrew Bible is a succession of episodes describing the development of a collective identity. Regina Schwartz, in her book *The Curse of Cain*,[5] has identified five particular modes in which identity manifests itself: covenant, territory, kinship, nation, and memory. It is amazing to realize how in a supposedly secular era the myth of monotheism still constitutes the basis of our notions of collective identity. I thought it useful to apply Schwartz's classification by taking a brief look at each of the aspects listed above and reflect on their implications.

Covenant

Israel's covenant with its God establishes that only the elected people can enjoy the benevolence and generosity of the deity. Divine resources are scarce and it will be only the chosen, i.e. *us*, who will benefit, not *them*, the idolatrous, those who have been abandoned and cursed by God for having shamefully preferred to worship spurious deities. With exclusivity comes *monolatry* (choosing the God of Abraham within the entire gamut of available deities) a term which is more accurate than *monotheism* (adherence to the ontology of a single God) in describing what occurs here.

Incitement to monolatry in *Deuteronomy* goes hand in hand with incitement to monogamy. Polytheism is compared to the abjection of sexual infidelity and promiscuity: the land of Israel is chastised by the deity because she behaves like a whore with other Gods, and the invectives reach fetishist paroxysm in Jeremiah who accuses Israel of committing adultery with pieces of wood and stone (Jeremiah 3:9).

The exclusivist deity of the Bible creates such demarcation from the beginning, preferring the offering of Abel to Cain's: God seems unable to bless both, and the same scarcity principle dominates the tale of Jacob and Esau: Jacob steals the blessing destined to his brother and for this reason becomes an exile.

One could object that such a climate of violence belongs to the Old Testament, and that the New Testament has brought us instead glad tidings of love. But is that really so? If the Old Testament annihilated otherness, the New Testament colonized it, or, euphemistically stated, converted it – hardly an improvement. I agree with Schwartz's hypothesis that the distinction ought not to be made in terms of Old or New Testament but in the direction of an interpretation of the Bible underlining, where possible, the metaphors of *multiplicity* and *plenitude* over the dominant ones of *oneness* and *scarcity*.

The promise of fertility, wealth and happiness which is to follow obedience to the covenant with the God of Israel does not materialize, while in Deuteronomy the list of curses, tortures and threats awaiting those who transgress the pact exceeds the blessings. To those who do not observe the clauses of the covenant, the tyrannical God grants a disastrous future: they will become an object of horror, the subject of cautionary tales; they will become proverbial or, literally, *a proverb*

(Deut. 28:37). The gravest transgression consists in spoiling – by worshiping another deity and/or having sexual congress with a foreigner – the identity of the community and its alleged solidity. Unlike the more rassuring avowal which associates monolatry to a moral code of universalism and peace, in the sacred texts we find the very opposite, i.e. defence of tribal prejudices. If any universalism is present, it is the universalism of totality and absolute truth, sole guarantor of a peace that already pre-dates *Pax Romana* and later *Pax Britannica* and *Pax Americana*: the universalism of empire, the moral law imposed by the colonizers.

Territory

How would we explain to an alien, Regina Schwartz asks, this peculiar habit of ours of building walls and fences, of planting banners and flags everywhere? How to explain that it is common practice for an invented, imaginary group (the nation) to obsessively want to possess a segment of the planet? How to justify that in the name of such an illusory notion millions of people have killed and have been killed? During the twentieth century two generations have been decimated for the sole aim of modifying a map: hard to explain to an alien that for us Earthlings life seems to be less precious than the soil.

Can a human being (by definition mortal and transient) truly *own* a territory? The promise of a land is, in the Bible, the unifying element of a people, provided they obey their God. To be human, *'ādām* in Hebrew, means to be made of soil, *'ādāmā*. The myth of the soil coincides with periods of history in which the people of Israel found themselves in exile, both voluntary (with the Exodus) and imposed (by the Babylonians). In spite of the fact that ownership of territory and exile are interdependent themes in biblical narrative and in spite of the equally relevant role played by nomadism, it was the theme of territory that prevailed in the end. Nomadism came to be understood retrospectively as penance and preparation before acquiring land ownership. With possession becoming a desirable condition, there are two alternatives: homeland or exile. Individuals who represent otherness, who have betrayed the community, are punished with exile. But what is exactly lacking in the exiled condition? And what is the difference between the wanderer, the tenant, and the owner?

The curse of exile can hypothetically metamorphose into the blessing of nomadic life, into the refusal to feed the false obligation of inhabiting a territory. Demarcation between those who belong to the homeland and those who are exiled from it can turn into the more pliable notion of the human being as transient, a visitor who receives the gift of a brief sojourn on the planet's crust. This is a poetic but also pragmatic stance. In biblical narrative, as soon as the land is owned, it fails to deliver its promise; borders must be protected, wars erupt with neighbouring tribes and systematic violations of God's covenant follow. Proud of having attained ownership, people cease to be faithful to their God. In the Bible, ownership of the land coincides with the spreading of idolatry[6]. Now that you had plenty to eat and have built beautiful dwellings, Moses admonishes, now that you possess gold and silver in abundance, do not become proud (Deut. 8:11–14). Could it be that the *promise* of a land is more important than its ownership?

Kinship

Once identity is defined in terms of possession, the history of a people becomes ensnared within the constrained narratives of invasion and exile, with the latter being background and justification for future conquest. This appears to be a recurring pattern, when we think of several configurations of oppression and conquest such as North America, or of German expansionism after the defeat in the First World War. In these cases the victim becomes perpetrator and creates new victims, a pattern sadly familiar to psychotherapists. The other interesting analogy is between the land and the female body, present everywhere in the Bible, founded on the idea of purity and contamination and on the intimate link between property of the woman's body in monogamy and possession of the elected people by their God in monotheism. Marrying a foreigner and creating an alliance with other tribes dirties the land, and the transgressor is evacuated and vomited out of it.

80

Condemnation of adultery is equally motivated by puritanical defence of the rigid confines of one's nation. *Zārā* is the excluded person, the foreign woman, archetype of the disorder of the senses and of social anarchy, a figure interestingly similar to Dionysus's female double, *Baubo*.[7] From his pulpit the biblical preacher thunders against the harlot, the adulteress, as well as against the man who joins a foreigner; in his invective the prophet mixes sexuality and possessions; the transgressor and the adulteress must be exiled. *Gala* in Hebrew means both an uncovered (unprotected) woman as well as an exiled one, a term expressing a prejudice against women and reinforcing exogamy as a taboo. It is difficult not to agree with Schwartz who sees in monotheism a doctrine of possession of a people by its God, of a land by its people, of women by men.[8] Even before being a sin in the sense ascribed to the word by morality, adultery and union with the foreigner transgress the law of property. Here too we see a paradox: encouragement to marry within one's own community, to delimit and possess, does not engender peace and happiness but violence, as attested by many biblical tales. In short, we kill in order to possess *and* because we are not able to possess. Even God, disappointed by their infidelity and refusal to be possessed, ends up killing his own people.

Unlike covenant and territory, kinship holds a certain prominence because it appears to be 'natural', somewhat providing evidence that identity has genealogy on its side. The people of Israel are described in the Bible as a great family, a clan whose paternity goes back to Adam, via a lineage going from father to father (and ignoring mothers), the aim of which seems to be deciding who belongs to whom. But is kinship really natural? According to anthropology, it is not, for it is nothing but a fiction.[9]

There are no doubt *ideologies* of kinship, notions guiding the structural narrative of the Bible, but alongside them we find numerous examples of the arbitrariness of kinship. Inheritance is stolen or violently assumed; brothers defraud one another, as do uncles and nephews in a climate of suspicion and cajolery where craving for ownership rules. Of course the emphasis on kinship still holds, directly proportional to the hatred and suspicion of the foreigner, translated as prohibition against exogamy. Endogamy provides of course its own set of fears and anxiety, above all the terror of dissolving identity. Yet one could almost say that for the Bible incest is the ideal form of matrimony.

Who is the stranger, from whose dangerous influence the clan must protect itself? The stranger is the *other*, i.e. one who is different from the *subject*. A non-poetic, non-ethical response to the stranger implies a politically reactive response to the asymmetry of encounter, hence to the problem of power. Subjugation, segregation, diplomacy, or aspiration to live alongside: these are some of the modalities of a political response, to which we can add new variations, including humanitarian wars on terror, an absurdity worthy of Jarry and Ionesco.

The theme of the rejected and disinherited son, of the son his father neglects in favour of his brother, often recurs in patriarchal narratives: Cain and Abel, Ishmael and Isaac, Jacob and Esau. The story goes on in contemporary sagas, in the familial feuds recounted in the therapy room, where one can hear the echo of Esau's imploration: "Do you only have one blessing, my father? Bless me too, my father!" (Genesis 27: 37–38), to which Isaac responds by confirming Esau's condition of exiled slavery and the chance of reprisal by means of rivalry and violence: "Behold, away from the fatness of the earth shall your dwelling be, and away from the dew of heaven on high. By your sword you shall live, and your brother you shall serve. But it shall come about when you become restless, that you will break his yoke from your neck" (Genesis 27: 39–40). Promises, blessings and preferential treatment of the chosen go hand in hand with curses, punishment, and exile for those who will not share paternal wealth and will be treated as foreigners and idolaters.

In the book of Ezra we find rabid xenophobia, inspired by the Leviticus notion of purity, by the fear of contamination by anyone who comes from elsewhere, whether Mesopotamia or Egypt, or from non-specific faraway lands. Protection of kinship means here protection from the *uncleanness* of foreigners and "their detestable practices" (Ezra 9:11).

What is the alternative to xenophobia? Some will say universalism, of the kind we find in the prophet Isaiah, the rhetoric of "we are all brothers, sons of the same father"; provided, of course, that the foreigners convert to the God of Israel. The doctrine of "we are all brothers" (and sisters), central in Christianity, easily turns into a doctrine declaring that *only* my brothers are human beings, while all others are representatives of inferior civilizations and as such must be treated.

Whether we are dealing with tribalism or universalism, xeno-phobia or globalization, the common effort is towards the creation of an identity, an attempt marked from the beginning by violence and the exclusion of otherness. The *other*, whose features and characteristics (ethnic, social and of gender) change with the changing of prejudices, remains always outside the walls of the *Polis*, no matter how vast its territory, whether outside a rural or a global village. One could of course quote *The Book of Ruth* as an example in the Bible where we find a foreign woman charitably nourished and protected, and later married, by an Israelite. At the end of the story, however, we learn that Ruth was not, after all, a foreigner.

The metaphor of the body associated with the notion of commu-nity is dangerous: the one body of community, alongside kinship and race, is an image too often used to dominate those who are not among the elected and to persecute those who are too easily identified with a particular 'race'. There are many examples in European history where both Jews and Catholics are conveniently labelled as 'race' and on that basis excluded from riches. The same goes for the ideology of colonialism which has with equal impunity fabricated notions of superiority and inferiority in order to justify slavery and barbarism. That the crimes of empire and colonialism have been perpetrated in the name of the Bible testifies both the cunning of delinquents in high places and that the Bible itself endorses violence perpetrated in the name of property and territorialism. In biblical tales and myths we find the very matrix of the division of humanity by global capi-talism into the two distinct *loci* of consummation/deprivation, development/under-development. To such primary division belongs the dichotomy, crucial since the emergence of the nation-state, between belonging and exile, between having a homeland and being stateless, having a dwelling and being homeless.

Nation

The typical individual of the modern era clutches on to the idea of nation.[10] Modern nationalism arises in the eighteenth century on the wings of a longing that could have been better sublimated into art, folklore and culture, but which found instead an outlet in this mystifying creation. In his seminal study Benedict Anderson sees the invention of the nation-state substituting for three essential entities which have vanished at the dawn of the modern era: (1) a language linked to ontology; (2) a hierarchical political organization clustered around a monarch; (3) a notion of temporality providing a cosmological and historical foundation[11]. Such notions were indispensable to survival in pre-modern times because they represented a safeguard against the dread of groundlessness and the dreaded meaninglessness of existence. The idea of the nation arose from the ashes of the theocratic era – a new fiction generating new certainties. Judging from the countless massacres perpetrated in its name, we must deduce that it enjoyed, and continues to enjoy, immense popularity.

Nationalism is an *invention* and not, as the rhetoric of national anthems would have it, the awakening of a people to self-knowledge.[12] An invention is both falsification and creation – in this case of an imaginary, invisible multitude whose presence emerges, diaphanous and unreal, to individual consciousness. The essence of a nation is twofold: all individuals within it have something in common, and each of them has forgotten many things. Brotherly embraces all-too easily overlook inequality and injustice, the exploitation of the oppressed and the corruption of the rulers. Nationalism has inherited both the biblical notion of territory and the hatred of the stranger which derives from it; its emergence coincided with the Enlightenment and the weakening of religious faith, providing a surrogate to faith and a substitute to both religious communities and to dynasties such as the Hohenzollern, the Ottomans, and the Romanov, which all became extinct after 1922.

This imagined society emerges in the ritual reading of the daily papers, in novels or in films where we follow 'our hero' in his adventures abroad, or during the ninety minutes of a football game where eleven over-paid youths invoke *l'elmo di Scipio* or *nos jeunes héros*, *our gracious Queen* or the supremacy of their particular assemblage *über alles*.

The nation-state requires adherence and loyalty in the name of a natural kinship that offers no other choice. *Heresy* literally means *choice* and against the danger of choice nationality is inculcated and 'naturalized' from birth alongside more obvious physical characteristics. In our allegedly natural ties we intuit participation in community and because not chosen these ties are endowed with a disinterested aura[13] which alongside the assimilation of language gives us an indelible *imprint.*

In the Bible the idea of nation is of a dynastic network with geographical, political and religious delimitations which enters into a pact of allegiance with a specific deity. The very identity of Israel is built against Egypt – the true nation worshipping the true God versus the false nation venerating the false God. The birth of the modern nation-state faithfully mirrored this ancient model.[14]

We often find within contemporary nationalist rhetoric a combination of ancient religious themes and modern positivist historicism bringing together the mythical patrimony of a people within the pseudo-concreteness of facts. As a result, an entire mytho-poetic and spiritual tradition is weighed upon a scale; this move is characteristic of fundamentalist thought, forever claiming to be able to fathom the unfathomable and quantify the unquantifiable, and is the expression of an *anti-aesthetic* mind, of a mind, that is, incapable of thinking the unconditioned and of suffering the conditioned.

The anti-aesthetic mind usually thinks of time in terms of linear development, with a focus on one imaginary goal.[15] A vision of time inspired by multiplicity would be made instead of fragmentary moments. We do find these in the Bible, but they have been systematized and made cohesively 'historical' by nineteenth century German historiography. For this tradition, from von Humboldt to Droysen, the task of the historian is to confer meaning and consistency to a formless and contradictory mass of events so as to trace the progress of the German nation. Applied to biblical studies, this perspective blends the ancient nation of Israel with nineteenth-century Germany. This predominant historical method is a traditional way of reading history – a history for historians which Foucault, inspired by Nietzsche, opposes to the effective (*wirkliche*) method of doing history.[16] While the former establishes a fictitious continuity, providing a foundation outside time and pretending to judge everything according to a sort of 'apocalyptic objectivity', the latter observes discontinuities and contradictions presenting an (anti) epistemological perspective underlining rupture rather than synthesis.

The Example of Israel

The creation of the state of Israel, inspired by Theodor Herzl's Zionist vision, offers us a more recent example of the creation of a nation-state and of its contradictions. It illustrates the problems of narrow religious identity and the dangers of messianism. Jacqueline Rose[17] has clarified the dangers of Zionist messianic fervour, exemplified in Herzl's mental instability, and in doing so she carries on a tradition of dissent within Jewish culture towards Zionism. Hannah Arendt had already perceived Herzl's messianic recklessness, while Buber had drawn a sharp distinction between a spiritual notion of Zionism and one of political supremacy which was detrimental to the Palestinians, and saw Israel's growing success as a disaster and a blatant example of prevarication. Differentiating between 'nation' and state', Buber asked, already in 1949: "Where is the nation inside the state? And where is the spirit of the nation?"[18] The creation of the nation-state with its multi-coloured knick-knacks – the flags, the slogans, the euphoric marches – and its prevarication of foreigners, sadly recreated those very same conditions from which the Jews had to flee. Just like that other illusory notion, the ego, nationalism confirms our delusion of self-sufficiency. But the very idea of autarchy is absurd. Herzl did not understand that the nation-state he yearned for was nowhere to be found, that there was no place on the planet where the organic body he envisioned – namely 'Jewishness' – could live. He failed to understand that a nation cannot develop within the walls of a collective biological entity.[19]

The destructive (and self-destructive) trajectory of the state of Israel (absolute faith in itself, hostility to the Arab world, self-sabotage, and commitment to the obliteration of Palestinians), is echoed in what took place in western democracies after 1989 and in the USA after 9/11: that crisis of 'auto-immunity' diagnosed by Derrida in *Spectres of Marx*.[20] The immune system that should keep at bay an infection or an enemy ends up summoning it and turns its weapons of defense against itself.

A group with an inflexible identity and an equally inflexible definition of the enemy creates its own environment and jargon, effectively manufacturing its own world. Much like a religious sect or an exclusive club, each group harbours madness in its centre: the internal boundaries give way ("we are all brothers and sisters united by the same faith") while the external ones harden against foreigners and enemies, against whom a historical vendetta is being enacted: it is the sad tale of every spiritual cult gathered at the feet of a guru or an individual who claims to have seen the light. It is also the sad tale, less detectable because more widespread and nearly ubiquitous, of nation-states and institutionalized religions.

Memory

Memory plays an important role in the creation of a nation state. What is memory? If we believe in the past as a solid entity, memory plays the part of a warden who from time to time opens the doors of the museum. Everything inside is made of ashes, but on our visits the warden reassembles the exhibit infusing life into the silhouettes and events which contributed to the creation of our identity. However, as soon as we stretch our hand to touch them, they turn again into ashes. Giving solidity to the past is not only futile; it also betrays the past. In individual biography, as in that of a people or a nation, defining a precise identity on the basis of the past is constructing a fiction on the basis of another fiction. To *delimit* the history of a people in the attempt to define its identity also delimits its cultural resources and their potential. Memory implies the opposite movement: re-membering is to rejoin creatively what has been dis-membered. It is an act of imagination –the province of the theatre more than the museum. The art of memory recreates what cannot be reconstructed or embalmed in the fixity of a past. In this way an individual and a people can re-interpret their past. It is possible to transform the past by transforming our relation to it. Each new interpretation – whether myth, biography, or sacred text – modifies its narrative and structure; in the multiplicity of interpretations, one affirms what I call *contemporary atheism*, the primary confutation of the One via a salutary descent into a myriad of perspectives, each of them valid in taking the past out of the museum and into the theatre, out of the mausoleum and into the uncertain light of the day.

This is also true, of course, for the Bible, as Schwartz rightly points out: Luther interpreted the Bible through his own belief that faith is itself promise of redemption; Milton saw it as affirmation of individual moral victories; Blake read the Bible as the epic of the oppressed imagination trying to free itself from the clutches of creation; Freud as the attempt on behalf of a primitive tribe to overcome parricide instincts.

Nationalism marries fate to contingency, creating the Frankenstein of *historical destiny*. This makes of an arbitrary community a nation pre-destined to glory (and catastrophe). Owing to imperial and colonial demands, and later to mass tourism, even some of the poor can afford to play at being lords and ladies. The settlers baptize the new cities with the name of their hometowns, fabricating simultaneity between the old and the new. The new ousts the old yet lives alongside it. Memory loses its character of longing and nostalgia and becomes artificial reconstruction of the homeland. The exile does not accept her condition but recreates a duplicate in artificial synchrony. She renounces the pain of separation but also the transformative power inherent in the exiled condition, i.e. the possibility of exit, from *ex*, the suffix common to experience, existence, and ecstasy: of being thrown into the vast world, into the gift/given of life itself.

To the English we owe the creation of a nation with imperial ambitions, imitated by successive bourgeois societies which in turn created the truly modern doctrine of the abstract and impersonal state.[21] It is important to remember that we deal with inventions: by introducing the state, modern nationalism has inherited and remodelled two centuries of transformations. Revolutionaries seizing power inherit the switch board of state control and a devilish bureaucracy and administration which is far from easy to dismantle.[22]

If the first nationalist movements were animated by revolutionary fervour, already the second generation of nationalism, during the European nineteenth century, grandly appropriates juridical rights of clairvoyance, with Michelet proclaiming that history is the supreme judge establishing justice even on behalf of the dead.[23] History would interpret (via the historians of revolution and nationalism) nothing less than the unexpressed desires of the millions of dead and miraculously speak in their place. Benedict Anderson wittily called it *inverted ventriloquism*. The idea of the nation is here linked to memory: one must remember or at least imagine the aspirations of past generations. Thus the colonialist who wiped out the indigenous traditions of oppressed and half-buried civilizations now exhorts others to nostalgia and exoticism. The injunction of memory is crucial in the building of individual identity as in that of a people, a nation or an empire. Memory being often unreliable, there is a constant need to narrate our individual history and that of the people we identify with, and this attempt is perhaps similar to emptying with our bare hands the floor of a sinking boat. Autobiography is an impossible battle against biology: the cells of the human body die and are replaced every seven years. The history of a nation must similarly create and recreate an artificial linearity which does not truly reflect the complex interpenetration of events. A nation too, precisely because intrinsically it does not exist, bears a desperate need to narrate itself into being, to manufacture a coherent storyline whose dates of conception, birth and death are arbitrary.[24]

The Name of the Other

Terrorist, illegal immigrant, asylum seeker, homeless: these are some of the contemporary names of otherness. The xenophobic epidemic in contemporary Europe feeds on blatant racism and turns it into 'reasonable' notions accepted by the once silent majority. "The best lack all conviction while the worst are full of passionate intensity" W.B. Yeats wrote, and his words still ring true today. The racist raises his voice while the law-abiding citizen nods and mumbles in his living room. Those who could act are incapacitated by a motivational deficit interpreted by Adorno as the inevitable consequence of modernity – not insurmountable but requiring an ethical stance which alone can revitalize politics. This is a difficult but necessary task which entails understanding the ethical sphere *outside* utilitarianism and morality, free from scientific induction and logical deduction. If ethics without politics is empty, politics without ethics is blind.[25] Introducing ethics in the alienated domain of politics brings about a critique from below of what is being imposed from above. It also incites the subject to *personal response*, and from this experiential dimension (*Erlebnis* more than *Erfahrung*) we can create the basis for a commitment that is not motivated by ideological loyalties but by a radical ethical response to the injustice and the violence of institutional power.

It is essential to free ethical and political commitment from conscience, liberal guilt and masochism. Nietzsche obligingly reminds us of that peculiar plant, bad conscience, growing in the psyche's foliage. We cannot ascribe ethics to guilty conscience. Western thought after Kierkegaard promoted a vision of interiority as atonement: one looks at one's soul in order to purify it of its mistakes. This in itself is a radical shift from the view of the self as a solid entity whose only way of pacifying anxiety is by subduing the non-self. But there is a small problem: interiority does not *intrinsically* exist; the subject is born when adequately responding to the event. Response to alterity is loyalty to the event, to the irruption of the Angel of Becoming in the nightmare of history. Such response is made possible by our recognition of the non-intrinsic existence of the self and the exceptionality of this embodied subject within the sea of phenomena.

We arrive at hetero-affectivity and the radically heteronymous perspective via studying the self through meditative practice, which is not introspection, atonement or relaxation but phenomenological investigation of *this*, the totality of the ineffable and undivided experience which unfolds as we speak.

Introspection, atonement, and relaxation are side-effects that must not distract us from the primary task of inquiry into the river of phenomena of which we are part. An ethical response inspired by such a mode of inquiry cannot but affirm our commitment to justice, for injustice is based on ignorance, on the superstitious belief in an acquisitive and fixed self. Without phenomenological inquiry, provided by meditative practice, ethical commitment easily slips into ideology. The diagnostic use of Marx must be juxtaposed to rigorous phenomenological enquiry established by meditative practice. The self can then be re-interpreted as *ethical subjectivity*.

We remain indebted to Hegel for his *socialization* of Kantian practical reason, while Heidegger's initial promising confutation of the solipsism of German idealism has been a disappointment, for it made us hope for an effective dismantling of Kantian subjectivity. Instead, it ended up substituting reason with a pre-rational domain and confirming the universality of being. What brings together Kant, Hegel and Heidegger is uninterrupted loyalty to the subject, neatly described by Critchley as the *orthodoxy of autonomy*.[26] Yet Critchley seems to have misunderstood the ineluctable presence of the *strange guest at the gate*, i.e. nihilism. Following Nietzsche's warning, nihilism cannot be sidelined but must be lived through. Any appeal to rebellious heteronomy which evades the confrontation with nihilism cannot but re-establish that very same orthodoxy of the idealist subject so skilfully refuted by Critchley. Things get more complicated when he recycles the Nietzschean expressions *passive nihilism* and *active nihilism*, attributing arbitrary meanings to them – respectively cynicism/passive pessimism and terrorist/revolutionary violence. The third option Critchley proposes is a form of ethical and political commitment inspired not by obligation but by desire for justice tempered by anarchic humour – a tantalizing suggestion. It is however important to clarify that passive nihilism is the nihilism of religion and of any system which, by repudiating the world, calls for a metaphysics. Active nihilism goes past these limitations; it welcomes the groundlessness of existence and creates meaning through an aesthetic move whose ramifications are ethical as well as political.

In the absence of a revolutionary subject (such as the proletariat before post-modernism), the urgent task is to *create* a subject, i.e. giving a name to a new transformative force, but this can happen only after having actively welcomed nihilism. God continues to be dead, and attempts at resurrecting Him have failed. Radical ethics arises from the divine carcass, from the decay of the transcendental but also of identity as we know it. Contemporary atheism arises from the ruins of metaphysics, from the recognition of our limited human power, and from integrity, understood as reluctance to use metaphysical shortcuts. This does not mean that no objectivity is possible unless one resides on the moon; it simply means abiding by a scientific, artistic and philosophical tradition demanding that we ask the fundamental question: "What can we *really* know?"

Wild Democracy

We turn to ethics not as a form of consolation after the disappointment with Marxism but because in ethics we recognize the missing
link without which politics is mere remixing of the bureaucratic
order and state administration. In ethics we find a response to specific
situations of injustice and violence. This is different from a turn
towards a vague spirituality, common among many of us who were
politically active in the nineteen seventies, a spirituality which found
an outlet in pre-established metaphysical systems and contributed to
a weakening of the Left.

Becoming apprentices of radical ethics means resorting to phenomenology rather than metaphysics and for this reason both *New
Age* spirituality and the Paoline, messianic visions proposed by philosophers such as Badiou and Žižek may be seen as totalizing
shortcuts. In affirming one's own loyalty to the event, the subject
comes to light; the creation of a truth emerges and dissolves in the
poetry of becoming, vital interlude to the prose of the world. The
emerging truth is impermanent: only a Platonic (Badiou) or
Hegelian (Žižek) can attribute permanence to the very idea of truth
– that very same idea in the name of which future oppression will
be established.

If disappointment with politics led some to spirituality, others
turned to passive acceptance of the *status quo*. But it also produced a
positive refusal of politics as careerism and a desire to find a motivation for ethical and political action in a radically changed scenario.
Activism today is manifold and never quite follows the orthodox
route: it goes from anti-capitalism to defence of the rights of indigenous people, from solidarity towards the homeless and 'illegal
migrants' to uprisings in the Arab world, from the vast ecological
movement to libertarian protest against the barbarism of proletarian
dictatorships which turned, as Bakunin predicted, into dictatorships
against the proletariat.

With the decline of the working class as the main social force in
post-industrial societies, the obliteration of the proletariat as revolutionary subject and the resulting disappearance of the primary
antagonism between the proletariat and the bourgeoisie, the task
today consists in articulating new subjectivities. In our post-modern

era, such articulation is necessarily *invention* rather than adjustment to pre-existing identities.

We have learned the hard way, yet with a sense of exhilarating freedom, the illusory nature of individual and collective identities: homeland, family, individual identity are impermanent and unreliable. The creation of new identities able to build new revolutionary subjects is not a rhetorical act but a deeply ethical one: commitment goes towards those who suffer more, who have lost all status and experience directly the existential uncertainty of the human condition, as well as the fatuity of social status itself.

In Marx's early works as in the notion of wild democracy enunciated by Merleau-Ponty we find a healthy scepticism towards the Hegelian notion of the state and a mode of thinking which encourages the building of an ongoing revolutionary and anti-state *momentum*. Rather than the appropriation of the state and its Kafkean apparatus, radical ethics creates an association of free human beings (*"einen Verein freier Mensche"* in the words of the young Marx). It affirms democracy as self-determination of the people (*Selbstbestimmung des Volks*), against and outside the state. A utopian notion, surely, but utopia is literally a non-place, from the Greek *ou* (non) and *topos* (place), a notion devoid of *locus* as well as *telos*; not a pre-established concept of social and political organization but ongoing anarchist opposition questioning any centralization of power.

From Critchley I borrow the twofold meaning of anarchism: (1) anarchism is *ethical* because devoid of *archè*, of the autonomous principle of the self; (2) it is *political* in the sense of responsibility towards the other. What differentiates this form of anarchism from its classical version is a greater emphasis on solidarity towards the other rather than on the autonomy of the self.

Some Marxist interpretations have been too deterministic in stressing economics and relegating the political, social and cultural dimensions to a rarefied 'super-structure'. Yet it is precisely in these domains that *hegemony* can be built. A civilization does not prevail in the long run because of its military might but thanks to the superiority of its culture. Global capitalism's economic and military power is ubiquitous; hoping that internal contradictions will automatically bring about its demise was the mechanistic view of the Second International, which dogmatized a notion explored by Marx

93

in the preface to *A Contribution to the Critique of Political Economy*.

We cannot neutralize the phony cosmopolitanism of globalization with the romantic ideal of all things rural and uncontaminated *à la* Scruton, but treasure instead our present dislocation and utilize it for the creation of a cultural hegemony. Gramsci's idea of hegemony embraces the contingent and dynamic nature of society, resisting the temptation to conceive the dominant ideology as static. For Gramsci, hegemony tends to the formation of a new common will uniting several groups and social strata: congruent to the Marxist project, it collectivizes the Hegelian ideal of inter-subjectivity.

For orthodox Marxism, Communism is understood as a metaphysical category prior to becoming or as the *telos* of history itself, rather than a creative, situational, and organized response to alienation and injustice. For this reason genuine and spontaneous movements of rebellion and transformation have been unrecognized and even reviled for not abiding by the script. The other problem is the question of universality: the revolutionary subject must embody the universal project of history: "I am nothing, and I must be everything" in Marx's own words. What I think is being asserted here is not ontology but the affirmation of human rights *by those to whom rights are denied*. From a place of lack comes the celebration of riches, from nomadic lives the joy of inhabiting the world, and from oppression our precious instinct of freedom. In setting the foundations of Gramscian hegemony, politics needs poetry; in order to create sublime fiction, a *metaphor of being* is needed, inspiring us to a more direct *perception of becoming*. The pervasive irony of our post-modern world is not a hindrance to ideals of justice and emancipation, but can be effectively used in order to temper totalitarian leanings.

It might seem paradoxical to resort to Marx, a thinker commonly interpreted as 'materialist' for an analysis of inter-subjective equanimity and its inherently spiritual characteristics. But Marx's materialism, often summarily execrated, must not be read ontologically, as metaphysical response to spiritualism but apprehended as the materialism of inter-subjective practice. Far from being an up to date version of Democritus's atomism, Marxism denounces the ubiquity of commodities and the alienated nature of social relations in bourgeois society. Marx does not stop here (if he did, Marxism would be a variation of Rousseau's sentimentality); he is also fascinated by the ruthlessness employed by capitalism in destroying every spiritual value in the name of capital. Nietzsche's statement *God is dead* did not actively kill the deity but merely registered the truth of groundlessness. Similarly Marx's materialism does not refer to *physis* but to the commodified nature of social relations. Integrated with contemporary ethics and its potential ability to heal us of our motivational deficit, Marxism can become a powerful transformative tool.

A return to politics needs to go through ethics – not as moralization of politics but as the ability to respond adequately and sensitively to injustice. By placing ethics before ontology, before morality, and before politics, we break political philosophy's vicious circle which from Plato to Hobbes has enslaved the individual to ipseity and its pre-ordained roles. We withdraw our preference for the privileged citizen, opening a gap in the walls of the *polis*. We learn again from non-citizens and non-persons the principles of democracy and human rights, how to put aside the obsolete notions of race, nation-state, and religious affiliation. We learn again what it means to be a *people*.

From our everyday life, ransacked and colonized by profit and greed, a real need emerges for justice and equanimity. This is the project of radical ethics, an invitation to transcend voluntary servitude and engage in acts of civil disobedience.

It is time to dispose of our dubious impulse towards cheap ecstasy and the consolatory quiver we feel when joining the patriotic choir. It is time to take a dignified distance from the grotesque bureaucracy of the state and the populist notion of the 'man in the street' in order to find a momentary dwelling in a new subjectivity. Power is built on the illusion of identity. It is possible to disentangle ourselves, through shared investigation, from the false need of projecting our notion of identity onto the institutions or to avoid the responsibilities of freedom by submitting to an external authority.[27] It is possible to purify current spirituality from the narcissism of 'self-improvement', the moralistic trap of interiority-as-atonement, and those relaxation week-ends after a week spent chasing after 'success'.

It is possible to direct intuitions acquired from genuine spiritual practice into the domain of ethics, building a political project based on its principles. After all, the combination of politics and ethics is not the brainchild of some extremist avant-garde but belongs to classic sociology, for it was Max Weber who identified the three fundamental qualities of a politician: passion, responsibility, sense of measure. Weber distinguished passion, understood as factual involvement with current issues (*Sachlichkeit*), from heatedness, and in vanity he saw the chief political enemy. What would Weber have thought of politics sliding into the realm of TV talkshows and managerial speak? Or of a situation in which what he called "the two mortal sins in politics", lack of commitment and lack of responsibility, have now become the rule? Weber wrote of vocation for science and vocation for politics, of giving oneself (*hingeben*), an act which is both passive and active, giving oneself freely to an urgent vocation. In order to do so, he admonished, it is necessary to be committed to an *ethics of responsibility* rather than an ethics of conviction. It is not enough for a leader to be convinced of the goodness of his ideas if history then proves him blatantly wrong. Weber calls such an attitude political infantilism.

The Spectre of Migrancy

A spectre is haunting Europe: the spectre of the migrant. Following the demise of the Soviet block at the end of the nineteen eighties, a growing number of people came to Western Europe and North America in search of a new life. They were greeted with cynicism, exploitation and hostility, all fed by an obscurantist ideology supported by the atavistic fear of the foreigner. The refugee has become a contemporary figure of hatred in our collective psyche, while at the same time we get teary-eyed watching TV documentaries on the plight of refugees of the past.

Nation-states have systematically ignored elementary human rights and abandoned the dispossessed to themselves. This is in their nature: for Max Weber the state is the only source of the 'right' to employ force, while experts and scholars from whom we expect objectivity behave like politicians, substantiating irrational and widespread fears and forgetting their responsibility as scientists. In his book *Globalization and its Discontents*, Joseph Stigliz, ex chief economist of the *World Bank*, quotes Pierre Bordieu, who admonished politicians in vain to behave more like scholars, committed to evidence based research. Instead the very opposite happens: scholars adapt facts to the ideas of those in power. Something similar happens with intellectuals whose duty is to give a critical appraisal of the situation and scrutinize the deeds of politicians. Instead they have by and large become mouthpieces of popular and governmental prejudices, especially since the mid nineteen eighties. Neither the Left nor the liberals have been able to respond adequately to the presence of the foreigner and to the questions posed by otherness. Both have proved incapable of dealing with the rise of xenophobia and the fundamentalist Right in Europe and the US. We are witnessing a sad decline of the intellectual, who is traditionally an *exile* (whether voluntary or against her will, whether metaphorically or geographically), one who is equipped to reveal uncomfortable truths, express untimely thoughts outside the orthodoxy and comfort of ministerial chambers. Contemporary intellectuals corroborate and ratify the fears and cruel prejudices of *doxa*, i.e. the common belief and public opinion substantiated by statistics, the colonized alienation of the 'man in the street'. But it was precisely an uncritical adherence to intolerance as well as hatred of alterity that encouraged the rise of Fascism and Nazism, more expressions of a national spirit in a crisis, attempting to recreate its identity by focusing on hatred of the Jews and the Gypsies, than mere products of collective aberration. Hatred of the foreigner has become a sport shared by all, cloaked by our ignorance of cultures we know little about.

It is surprising and worrying that well known writers ritually join the choir of prejudice: a choir of clichés, a witch hunt directed at the public enemy, whether Islamic, refugee or deviant – very useful in reassembling the fiction of the nation-state. Yet this idea is based on the alleged superiority of one's own culture and civilization over the culture and civilization of the other, an attempt to inject life into the clay Golem of national spirit and cement our idolatrous attachment to the soil.

Immigration gives citizens of any nation the opportunity to assess the degree of civilization, culture and humanity we have achieved, for culture and formative education are not maieutics – i.e. the act of giving birth to pre-existing ideas – but openness to a genuine impact with exteriority. Isolationism engenders narrow-mindedness and prevents the development of *culture* which always emerges from the encounter and the medley of peoples rather than the primitive defence of a territory we believe to be ours. The Schengen agreement of 1985, launched by France and Germany and inspected by the European police and a group of defence ministers, ratified such an ignorant stance: on the one hand it abolished transit restrictions of European citizens within the EU, on the other it effectively denied access to foreigners, relegating Italy, Spain and Greece to the slavish role of Europe vigilantes in exchange for membership of the European club. The essence of European culture is being ridiculed by such philistinism. The art and high culture of Europe, since its dawn a complex melange, is made up of the works of exiles. Without exile and migration there would be no European culture.

We see here re-enacted in the social sphere what we have witnessed among peoples in the name of defence and acquisition of territory since biblical times: the aggressor appears as victim and attributes guilt to his victims. It will then be the task of self-proclaimed defenders of a wounded society to sanctify violence against deviants, heretics, gypsies or migrants, in accordance with the dishonourable tradition of finding internal and external enemies of the nation-state. Nazism and Fascism are in this context only the extreme outcome of a tendency which civil society has never entirely abandoned. Fear feeds on the irrational hatred of the stranger, with media and government transmuting the subjective trepidation of the 'man in the street' into a generalized, permissible terror. What is the citizen afraid of? And why is he so ready to take justice into his own hands? Because the territory is in danger: defense of territory is an atavistic reaction which snubs diplomacy and subtlety and demands the annihilation or ejection of those perceived as enemies: in an era where the ethico-political matrix of human solidarity collapses, generic appeals to morality allow a pretence of humanity and a distance from more extreme intolerance. To this purpose the definition of what constitutes a crime is liberally extended to include *infringements* ('illegal immigrants' washing car windows at the traffic light) and *victimless crimes* (prostitution and the purchase of drugs for private use) in order to punish deviancy – a term increasingly associated with migrants.

We are All Inauthentic Refugees

Philip Marfleet recounts his first visit, in the nineteen seventies, to Nabatiyeh, an encampment of Palestinian refugees who lived in Galilee but had been forced to flee north in 1948 following the conflicts immediately after the creation of the state of Israel. Returning twenty five years later, he found only a few of the people still there; the majority had been forced to flee and be uprooted again because of bombardments.

In the light of the suffering of millions of people the optimism of globalization apologists sounds grossly inappropriate. There are those who theorize the clash of civilizations and hypothesize an acceleration of the conflict between 'our' way of life and 'theirs', between the West and the Islamic world – a theory breeding catastrophic results through the recent 'war on terror'. The naïveté of some statements would make one smile if it were not for their toxic implications, with their mixture of obscurantism and hatred of otherness, as in the case of Samuel Huntington, who eulogizes globalization and argues that with the end of the Cold War important differences between peoples became cultural, centred around the question "Who are we?", to which people apparently respond by defining first and foremost their enemies. The psychoanalyst Hannah Segal wrote of the dangers of such paranoid views at the time of the end of the Cold War: the West would be unable to manage without manufacturing an enemy. Surely enough some years later Huntington identified the West and the Islamic world as two monolithic blocks clashing like characters in a cartoon, a view that, as Edward Said pointed out, ignores the pluralist and contradictory dynamics within these two worlds. Huntington's position draws on the work of British orientalist Bernard Lewis, author of the unequivocally titled *The Roots of Muslim Rage*, a leading exponent of a tradition which continues to produce bad history, actively fomenting and legitimizing ideas echoed in apocalyptic video-games and the pronouncements of ignorant leaders.

After the end of the Cold War, widespread hostility towards migrants and refugees provided western states' strategists with a new brand of public enemies to be placed beside Islamic terrorism and international crime as well as new justifications for the increase of draconian security norms. In the meantime the Third World, unconvinced by the fervent chorus of globalization, has been declared unqualified and dysfunctional, given that not only it declines to join, at its own expense, the corporations' binge party, but continues to secrete millions of refugees creating serious problems for rich countries, forcing them to permanently file 1.3 million people, as in the *Schengen Information System*, thus violating human rights in the name of security.

By the end of the nineteen nineties it became obvious that the exclusion, dislocation and suffering of billions of people did not match the universal wellbeing prophesied with the advent of globalization. It became clear that the universalism, cosmopolitanism and multi-culturalism flaunted by politicians and eulogized by intellectuals of the Left and of the Right merely corresponded to the freedom without frontiers of capital and profit. Frontiers were indeed open to the corporations but not to the free travel of people. In the name of profit for oligarchies within nation-states, we turn a blind eye to those who cross the frontier; we benignly tolerate low-cost labour from non-citizens prepared to do what no citizen is prepared to do – a symptom of false tolerance which confirms exclusion. In the name of profit we create artificial distinctions between genuine and non-genuine refugees, between the talented professionals and the poor and desperate deviants. The market is free and the market calls the shots, while the state unashamedly bows to its decrees; the market is free and it needs slaves and scapegoats, while the state and its 'intellectuals' supply targets for giving vent to the recurring fears and the ire of self-righteous citizens.

Does the state truly represent the interests of its citizens? Is the state truly capable of mediating the interests at stake? Or does it blindly serve the interests of capital? It is legitimate to ask whether the control of people's movement by the state is justifiable and whether the exclusion of non-citizens in the name of security is ethical. It is time to support the cultural, ethical and political movement in favour of a different globalization, via the identification of us citizens with refugees and migrants. Only then we can truly call ourselves citizens rather than mere bourgeois, for a citizen is one who can respond ethically and responsibly to the presence of otherness, whereas a bourgeois is one who builds around the ego citadel the walls of his own prison. Who is a resident and who is a migrant in the midst of impermanence? Who can claim ownership within a reality which, as the Buddha teaches, has no foundation but is incessantly renewing itself?

We allow entry to 'genuine' refugees, and the 'inauthentic' are sent back or incarcerated while their authenticity is being verified. The Heideggerian irony of this situation is irresistible: we are all inauthentic. Humans are, as anthropology, philosophy, psychology and biology all teach us – *inherently inauthentic*. To be human is precisely to inhabit such ambiguity, to reside in the impossibility of synthesizing vital functions with individual history, of matching the real with the ideal.

Legality and Illegality

Saying *welcome* is an act of arrogance. The territory does not belong to us. We are but tenants on the crust of the blue planet – a fleeting presence whose task is perhaps weaving a net of solidarity with fellow travellers.

Our welcome to professional and well-mannered refugees, to migrants who submit to integration and the learning of our idiom is bogus. The category of 'refugee' is mutable – applied and modified at will by politicians and motivated by our need to define a national identity which in our heart we know to be fragile.

The very demarcation between authentic and inauthentic refugees betrays the suspicion that the great majority of them might be 'illegal', but illegality is a double-edged sword. European and north-American history is full of examples of illegal networks of migrations created by the nation-states themselves: the escape of Calvinists from France in the seventeenth century; the escape of thousands of people using clandestine networks following the revolutions at the end of the eighteenth century; the victims of Fascism who in the twentieth century payed secret agencies in order to be expatriated. Each of these examples was later commended as showing heroism and inventiveness in the face of adversity. In 1946 the Truman administration organized *Operation Paperclip*, a clandestine transportation to the US, with fake visas and forged documents, of dozens of Nazis from Germany, together with collaborationists residing in Eastern Europe and in the Baltic countries. Many of these were scientists, whose expertise the USA intended to employ. When the entire operation was exposed, Truman justified his actions by saying that these people were 'freedom fighters' whose skills were going to be useful against the danger of Communist Russia.

It was a vast clandestine traffic of mass migration, organized by the Zionist movement, to transport 70,000 Jews into Palestine, later celebrated as heroes and pioneers. In the nineteen sixties the USA organized the illegal expatriation of Cuban citizens, a shrewd manoeuvre of negative propaganda against Cuba, particularly interesting if we consider the later labelling of these same Cuban citizens as 'illegal'. At the end of the nineteen eighties many exponents of the democratic movement in China reached the then British colony of Hong Kong, with the help of criminal networks and were praised as heroes of democracy. When a while later other members of the democratic movement reached by their own initiative the north-American shores, they were sent back by the Clinton administration because they were said to constitute a danger to security.

Open Borders

It is precisely when faced with a difficult situation that we must be able to think the unthinkable. This is the task of radical ethics. Radical ethics is not *realpolitik*, compromise with the powerful, defence of the privileges but unconditional solidarity towards the oppressed, since only by doing so can a human being be truly human, and the citizen can be a citizen. What is the unthinkable in the context of the nation-states and the refugees they engender? It can be expressed in two words: *open borders*.

There is a new activism at work, criticized by all politicians, yet responding in an engaged way to the mounting wave of racism and exclusion which has grown steadily in Europe and North-America since the end of the nineteen eighties and which demands the *abolition of border controls*. Programmes of deportation have everywhere grown in number; in countless centres of detention, migrants are kept in inhuman conditions, guilty only of not having the right papers: one more attestation of the fact that immigration control, racism and exclusion are inseparable. Is such a demand for open borders utopian? In the case of borders and migration, such a demand is a radical response to suffering and exploitation; it is a form of active defence of human rights targeting the arbitrary nature and the inherent violence of the notions of territory and of nation-states. As in the anti-war movement, the movement for open borders questions the right to hate the other and affirms the crucial element of difference and of encounter between cultures as necessary to the advancement of human progress. As Marfleet points out, war mobilizes 'us' versus 'them', manipulating feelings against external enemies. The anti-war argument and the fight against poverty and epidemics have won much support over the years; it is now time to submit migration control to the very same scrutiny. This is even more urgent as European attitudes to immigration since the 1990s have taken a sharp turn towards intolerance, with host cultures feeling free to speak against migrants in a misguided attempt to protect European values against the perils of multiculturalism. EU's member states' escalating hatred of migrants no longer allows for their disdain of South Africa's xenophobia.[28]

The mythologies of fear and suspicion often portray the migrant as weak and ailing, even evil and deviant. Yet the lives of refugees and migrants continue to testify throughout history the courage, initiative and inner resources of human beings when faced with the adversities of fate and the cruelty of their fellows.

III

DWELLING POETICALLY ON THIS EARTH

Of Ethics as a Branch of Aesthetics

Ethics originates within the observation of phenomena, hence it is inscribed within the practice of phenomenology, which teaches us that perception and appreciation of contingency is a poetic act. Husserlian essences manifest poetically as images, placing aesthetics at the very heart of science – perhaps akin to *haiku* poetry more than to explanatory formulas. *Dwelling poetically on earth*: Hölderlin's phrase implies celebrating the tragic and transient nature of existence, and affirming the impossibility of owning anything[1]. Variously interpreted by poets and philosophers[2], to this writer the verse expresses an appreciation of becoming without manufacturing being behind the curtain. She interrupts the self so as to be able to host the other and be transformed by its presence. Unconditional hospitality is vulnerability, disclosure of our inalienable solitude, elegiac tenderness which makes friendship possible.

Besides being a poetic act, unconditional appreciation of the contingent nature of existence follows the historicist teachings (forgotten by Husserl) of both Vico and Hegel. It is again to *art* that we must turn, rather than psychology or sociology, for examples of this stance: the prose of Virginia Woolf escapes solidification, affirms the ephemeral beauty of existence, dewdrops on the morning grass. Art shows the fundamental principles of phenomenology. Awareness of phenomena liberates us from the Cartesian/Freudian psychic apparatus; it alerts us to the fluidity of the self and the presence of the other.

It is my aspiration to be human that makes me respond to the other, rather the suggestions of psychology, telling me that the other is similar to me, or the intimations of science, inviting me to study her characteristics. I respond because this is the only way I can accept the invitation of becoming, that is, the invitation of poetry. By responding, I join humanity. Lovers know this space intimately, at least in the beginning: the beloved opens me up to exteriority and infinity. Later, when the instant becomes sequence and a fellowship contract, the other may even *preclude* infinity – unless we have a discipline at our disposal, an affirmative aesthetic practice keeping the doors of perception open without resorting to religion or drugs. This discipline is meditation, which can be seen as a kind of affirmative art. The courage necessary for dwelling poetically on this earth emerges from the understanding of the irreversibility of time and of life itself as temporality. A non-poetic mind will opt for the pseudo-solutions of religious dogma and scientism while a coarse mind will resort to the bitter consolations and the despondency of cynicism.

The ethical condition registers the tension between the poetic dimension and observance of the law. The former comes out of love, out of the capacity to forgive, appreciate beauty, and be moved by grace. The latter is the defensive hyper-rationalism of the bourgeois who has introjected the norm. The ethical life is *paradox*, intuitive response, beyond the prejudice of doxa, to the unremitting process of destruction and creation. Time is not *res*, nor a datum; it flees, evades. For Virgil, the best days flee earlier on in life. For Bergson, salvation consists in our ability to recognize the *instant*, an occurrence of an order different from being. In the instant, transformation is possible, provided we are able to attend without resorting to rational defences. John Keats famously called this faculty *negative capability* – the threshold of an enigmatic, ordinary revelation – not an automatic event but one that is co-created. Having come to such a threshold, transformation is possible: who I was until then vanishes: another *I* comes to light. In the instant, I am able to give myself unconditionally. In this sovereign act, the invisible, hidden within the interstices of the everyday, becomes visible. Generosity is then possible, giving what one is not, giving precisely because the I is incapable of giving. This is not John Stuart Mill's utilitarian principle nor Kant's categorical imperative, nor a deed following the Platonic contemplation of the Good. It is a free action, that is, a poetic action.

Of Religion as Bad Poetry

Ethics is poetry and as such it is inspired by the Muses rather than the Sirens. Orpheus's lyre spurs us to generous, hence ethical and poetical, deeds. The arguments of Aristotle, Augustine and de Sade lead us instead to Manichean universes. The Muses, daughters of Mnemosyne, remind us of the path of individuation, whereas Sirens divert us towards inconsistency and mummification, both characteristic of puritan rationalism. *Cave carmen*, they warn us, beware of the song. We must surely question music's charm, its persuasive power seducing us towards sentimentality. At the same time we must be able to doubt the puritan frigidity which macerates the seed of poetry hence the very possibility of ethics. Ethics is an interrupted serenade, a declaration of love refusing final consummation and the annexation of alterity into ipseity. It refuses it not out of moral condemnation of Eros but because, with the anxiety of non-being accepted and transmuted our habitual need to fill lack through engulfment is substituted with the celebration of *encounter*, an event which might be called *miraculous* because inscribed in uniqueness and temporality. The miracle occurs within the instant and breaks the natural relation between things. For the Hegel of *Philosophy of Reason*, miracle is "violence against the spirit". It is also violence against moralizing duty, for it opens us to non-linear perception, incomprehensible to the categorical imperative. It does not occur *outside* phenomena nor is immersed within becoming. And what is becoming but a constant miracle? But the amount of courage a human being can summon only allows sporadical forays into *becoming* – hence our predisposition to build instead clay dwellings within *history*. The miracle is then lived as fortuitous event, twist of fate, throw of the die. No one can inhabit such a dimension permanently, not even those whom a certain spiritual rhetoric likes to call 'enlightened'. Return to perceptive discontinuity, to the domain of Cartesian separation is inevitable and, in a sense, a relief. Sheltering from bad weather, from the unbearable beatitude of the *instant*, the subject finds solace in the solitude of separate existence from where she can reconfigure infinity and recompose the longing, or compose a song to the Impossible.

Moving freely between the instant and the interval, the poet/philosopher is no longer subdued by the Socratic tedium of knowledge-as-virtue. Already Spinoza unceremoniously divests us of the Socratic illusion according to which nothing bad will ever happen to the virtuous. The poet/philosopher is no longer a vassal of the goddess of reason, of the exclusivist God of the Bible, and of neo-Buddhist fatalism. She can breathe the salty air signaling the vicinity of the sea. In order to access this vision she must commit multiple transgressions, the most outrageous of which (given that her medium is philosophy) is the refusal to attribute primacy to reason, to obey an injunction which dominates western thought throughout its history, from Socrates and Aristotle to Augustine and Kant and includes the hyper-rationality of much post-modern thought. For Aristotle knowledge is universal and necessary; for Kant reason seeks universal and necessary judgment; Socratic not-knowing itself ends up confirming, in a gesture of consummate theatricality, blind faith in universal knowledge, for only one who sees a source of truth in knowledge can declare not to know anything.

Both enslavement to reason and dependence on religious beliefs are ways of abdicating the freedom which is instead affirmed through poetry, art and meditation. Socrates and Plato disdained artists and poets because the truths they reveal are not gifts of the goddess of reason but artefacts product from ambiguous sources. These sources were accessible to Hellenic wisdom before Socrates – to thinkers such as Heraclitus, to poets and playwrights of the tragic era, but no longer within the reach of Socrates.

Shestov did find similarities between the poetic revelations of pre-Socratic Hellenism and the religious revelations of Isaiah and St Paul, but I am inclined to believe that there *is* a great difference between the two, which is the gap between poetry and instituzionalized religion. From William Blake we learn that poetic intuition remains fluid in art but becomes crystallized in religion. Strong poets like Dante, Milton or Blake are essentially founders of individual religions without followers, creators of myths singly distilled by experience. Isaiah, Paul, and Kasyapa in Buddhism are instead founders of institutional religions, that is, creators of bad poetry. Religion is bad poetry, translation *ad litteram* of the mystery of existence, intrusion of reason and of tribal politics within the domain of the ineffable.

From the contemplation of impermanence, Heraclitus extracts sublime poetry: impossible to manufacture a new cathechism from his ambiguous fragments. From the contemplation of the finitude of life, Paul erects instead the foundation of Constantine's future imperial domination.

A disciple of Heraclitus, that is, one who is able to accept becoming actively, cannot be contented with the rational certainty of Socrates, nor with the irrational certainty of Paul: she might walk along the path of *faith* but without the reassuring conclusions of dogma and revelation. A difficult position, which some disciples of Heraclitus were unable to sustain, opting instead for the religious surrogate of a neutral *Dasein,* eternally stuck between an introspective impotence and the endorsement of barbarism. It is almost impossible to encounter becoming without resorting to forms of substantiality stolen from the realm of necessity.

Heidegger doubtlessly anchored his thought in facticity and conceived ontology as hermeneutics of factual life. Yet he saw in the *fall* (in the way in which the subject finds itself existing in a particular situation, tied to fatality and decline) the crucial configuration of facticity, rather than in the arbitrary contingency according to which we could be *elsewhere* and *otherwise*. What is given to us can be transformed into a creative task, but in the Heideggerian fall, the human being finds himself instead inextricably confined to the body, biology and history in the lethal identification which is one of the characteristics of Hitlerism. Imperious needs of the blood, ancestral calls to heredity and the past, the inevitability of biology all chain us to matter – primitively understood as mere materiality. By misunderstanding facticity as enchainment to materiality (rather than appreciating it as arbitrary and miraculous contingency), the destiny and essence of human beings is apprehended as slavery, a form of slavery which is different even from the firm disposition of souls in Dante's hell, where the acquisition of a *habitus* is not enchainment but residue of fate as well as imprint of the individual will.

To welcome matter passively, to even take delight in one's enslavement within the confines of an eternally recurring hellish circle is far from the acceptance of death and finitude, to genuine overcoming of one's attachment to power and domination.

Of Trivial Discourse

Ethics, like poetry, is the opposite of triviality. In pre-modern China the term *xiaoshuo,* literally 'trivial discourse' was used to indicate narrative and prose writing as distinct from poetry. The modern usage of the term includes superficiality, arrogance, and egotism. It is both an aesthetic and ethical category – giving in to *bad taste.* The response to the ethical demand posed by alterity manifests in the domain of the *immediate*, well beyond the suspicion of Kierkegaard who saw the shadow of egotism lurking behind it. Immediacy is enthusiasm for life, immersion in work and love yet without the illusion of doing something heroic and self-important. Kierkegaard's Christianity becomes ascetic precisely because he does not make such a distinction. But it is possible to live fully without being an egotist, and to be a fully detached egotist. It is possible to experience sexuality without being pulled down into ignorance, and it is possible to practice a form of self-righteous, lusty abstinence.

Fragmentation is not a New Canon

It could be objected that by stating that ethics derives from aesthetics we would risk reducing the sheer gravity of the ethical dilemma. But the crucial link with aesthetics and art liberates ethics from its millennial dependence on totality.

In *Minima Moralia* Adorno, later echoed by Said, dwelled on the music of late Beethoven, an artist who in the presence of death proclaims the impossibility of artistic synthesis and whose last musical production emerges as lost totality and fragment. It is no coincidence that Beethoven's late compositions gave Virginia Woolf the rhythmic inspiration for *The Waves*, a work of incomparable grace which can be read as a classic of phenomenology.

Yet we must refrain from elevating the fragmentation we find in Beethoven into a new code, as it happened via the orthodox disso-

110

nances of the new music that followed. We should see it instead as authentic loss, as a song breaking out in the presence of the ineffable.

Like art, ethics reflects the dilemma of responding to experience without manufacturing systems of consolation. Via ethics we rescue individuality, through voluntary exile and engaged noncompliance to a totalizing ethos. From Genet we learn the importance of betraying a cause; we learn the primacy of silence over logos, of perpetual rebellion over an abstract common good. We learn to see that collective revolutions will inevitably metamorphose into another form of oppression of individuals, of those artists and intellectuals who had championed the revolution out of love rather than through the accident of nationality and the dictates of ideology. We learn that functionaries and politicians act solely in order to maintain their privileges.

Heretical Love

Genet is in love with the other, the stranger, the pariah. He chooses as a concrete symbol of his rebellion the Palestinian cause, providing it does not crystallize into a new identity. Perpetual rebellion impairs identity; it unmasks it as a psycho-socio-political imposition. Identity is at the heart of imperialism; it is in fact, as Edward Said wrote, what imperialism exports. Genet's experience is exemplary; in him we find the *visceral love* that justifies a different form of universality by means of dislocation – a nameless, lawless, yet redeeming love which finds its political equivalent and supreme symbol in the Palestinian cause. This position is still compelling when one reflects on the fact that Palestinian identity is to this day universally criminalized and identified with terrorism.

Genet's example is remarkable in another way. His natural nomadism and rebellion do not become derailment of the senses nor are they translated into a portrayal of evil among velvety and comfy pillows *à la Baudelaire*. It finds its natural place in rigorous thought and exact language, unflustered and tender in the midst of despair. If his love for the dispossessed is personal and subjective, his love for revolution is universal and objective. He envisioned revolution as the tail of a tiger who is about to leap. As with Pasolini, Genet's love for

111

the revolution is heretical, contradicting all fashionable discourse and risking anachronism through its sheer intensity. Perpetual rebellion manifests secretly, disseminated both within and outside politics.

Golden Resin from the Tree of Knowledge

The curbing of social unrest is today entrusted to underpaid regiments of counsellors whose training brings together cognitivism, behaviourism and *New Age* obscurantism. The hope is that some distilled wisdom-while-u-wait will appease the unruly and drag them back to their reserved seat in the traffic jam. Counsellors and psychotherapists can nevertheless realize the genealogy of their profession and subvert its aims. One of the ways in which this subversion can take place is through the ancient practice of outspokenness or *parrhesìa*, the Greek notion revisited by Foucault. In the style of the cynic school, *parrhesìa* is often transgressive and provocative, an open challenge demonstrating that a true sovereign is not one who has managed to occupy a throne via political manoeuvering but one who has the courage of his ideas.

An ancient parable of such a spirited stance – essential to those who practice philosophy outside bourgeois illusions – is the meeting between Diogenes and Alexander the Great. Diogenes was sunbathing naked on the beach and commanded Alexander, who had gone to greet him, to move away because he was obstructing the sun rays. An example of *parrhesìa* was the rebellion of Buddhist monks in Burma, an exceptional event when we consider the obeisance often shown by Buddhism towards totalitarian regimes.

In ancient Greece we find myriads of examples, each of them showing the courage of philosophers against established power, a courage corroborated by the conviction of being on the side of truth. The *absolute* character of such truth is not given by its objective value but by the simple fact of uttering something dangerously different from the opinions supinely accepted by the majority. Expressed from the bottom up, parrhesìa weighs up the sovereign. By definition a hierarch cannot exercise parrhesìa; a person in power might be able to play the parrhesiastic game if he or she has overcome narcissism – a rare case indeed, for the greed and hypocrisy indispensable to occupy a position of power are at variance with the practice of parrhesìa. The other reason why the truth proposed by *parrhesìa* rarely fails to convince is that, far from being the logorrhea unleashed by the semi-literate gossip of *Facebook*, the 'public intimacy' of the artist displaying details of her love life in a public gallery or the manipulative rhetoric of the latest populist leader, parrhesìa is the result of *epimeleia heautou*, the *care of self* which is a philosophical, aesthetic and ethical discipline.

In Euripides' *The Phoenician Women* Jocasta meets her exiled son Polinices, who tells her that he suffered most from being deprived of the freedom of speech and from having to tolerate the idiocy of rulers. In *The Trojan Women*, Cassandra harshly criticizes the king's messenger as a lackey, a mere servant of the powerful. The exercise of parrhesìa, of open critique of hierarchy helps democracy and invites exchange within a community. Yet frankness is not enought; parrhesìa differs from mere chatter by being grounded in ethics. In the fourth book of his *Nicomachean Ethics*, Aristotle sees care of self as an attribute of the magnanimous person – far from the Christian notion which sees it as redemption from sin. After two thousand years of Judaeo-Christian influence it might be impossible to conceive of such a notion in the Hellenic sense, yet Foucault found in it the inspiration to formulate his fertile idea of *subjectification*.

Falling Creates God

Within radical ethics the idea of redemption is subverted. In Clarice Lispector's novel *An Apple in the Dark*, the protagonist Martin is able to *create* God because he is a fallen human being. Through his fall he creates himself and then creates God. It could well be that because confrontation with the reactive nihilism inherited by the Judaeo-Christian tradition is inevitable, the fall must be confronted from within rather than resorting to external mythologies. Yet the Greeks continue to inspire us with their insistence – reverberating through Goethe, Nietzsche, Foucault and many others, on the intimate link between ethics and aesthetics, as well as on the hidden harmony between *logos* and *bios*.

Harmony between saying and doing, between what one discusses

113

and how one lives is musical harmony, more precisely *Doric* harmony, a favourite of Plato who for various reasons despised other harmonic modalities. He scorned the *Phrygian* because it was associated with the passions; the *Ionic* because he thought it too solemn. But to arrive at such harmony implies a conversion, a transformation in the way of being and thinking, in one's *style of life* as Adler would say, something which I believe is partly betrayed by the Socratic/Platonic solution with its appeal to reason.

It is through the Epicurean thinker Philodemus that parrhesìa becomes an art – similar, according to Foucault, to the art of the doctor and that of the helmsman, an art characterized by awareness and, as Democritus said, by *timeliness*: not mere freedom of expression but the wisdom to discern the right moment for expression.

The Art of Friendship

From the Epicurean *ekklesia* we learn the art of friendship, crucial for the creation of a *temenos*, of a Buddhist *sangha*, of any cohesive, non-hierarchical group of explorers and experimenters. In such a community the individual finds a fertile soil for friendship, for the more nurturing aspect of the care of self which has its counterpart in contemplative practice and solitude. The Hellenic influence would benefit western Buddhist communities as these are mostly founded on hierarchies, on a passively accepted tradition of received wisdom, on those surrogates that Karen Horney used to call "glory systems". They mostly reproduce Judaeo-Christian frames of reference rather than being inspired by the egalitarian, experimental ethos of a proper *ekklesia*. The Hellenic influence would perhaps also debunk asceticism and moralism – two dominant forms of life denigration – and reconfigure them as *study of self* and *mastery*, ways in which the individual reconsiders his/her faults directly, rather than giving in to a paralyzing, melodramatic guilt.

Daimon and Anti-daimon

For Seneca non-virtue is inefficiency in coordinating one's behaviour rather than the transgression of divine law. The self-scrutiny advocated by the Stoics (think of Epictetus, who suggests that we should scrutinize sensory impressions in the same way we check the authenticity of a coin) is a courageous act which reminds one obliquely of public scrutiny – never feared, according to Robespierre, by a true revolutionary.

The decisive element in such an attitude comes yet again from art rather than morality or politics. Plutarch quotes the example of the painter who from time to time examines his unfinished painting from a distance. Similarly the person committed to the care of self distances himself from absorption and excessive familiarity with the self and, noticing discrepancies in his nature, learns to accept and modify them. The *humus* which makes us humans is a soil to be cultivated rather than mud and dirt from which we avert our gaze in search of transcendence.

Already in the nineteen fifties Maslow, drawing on Kurt Goldstein's work and anticipating ideas which were to be essential for the heretic psychotherapy of years to come, underlined the basic unity between the noblest and the most basic impulses. He stressed how the link between individuality and civilization had to be reconfigured, overcoming the Freudian prejudice of civilization's discontents. If there is harmony between the gratification of pleasure and the cultivation of noble impulses, Maslow maintains, then spontaneity and liberality rightly displace repression, self-control and discipline. The very concept of civilization is then modified to mean forms of *synergy* rather than dependence on hierarchies and revealed truths. Human nature – organismic, biological (though not limited by and least of all explained by biology) – contains the way out of key ethical conundrums. The organism itself expresses needs and values, and becomes sick when deprived of them. The basic unity between good and evil will later be creatively developed by Rollo May and by his notion of the *daimonic*.

If the *daimon* is hard to define, we nevertheless know all too well what constitutes the anti-*daimon*: apathy, absence of pathos and perhaps absence of pathology, given that pathology (from *pathos*, passion) is what makes us human. For May the daimonic is any natural function which has the power of taking over the individual; dangerously close to psychosis yet intimately linked to creativity.

115

Not unlike Socrates' daimon, yet irreducible to the voice of conscience, if by this we mean the introjections of social conditioning, the Freudian super-ego, or Heideggerian contemplation.

Good and evil live together in the organism as generative forces, as vagabond and winged energies threatening to overwhelm the person. One can use morality as a method for taming these energies or resort instead to ethics in order to realize their power.

Care of self may lead one to uncharted territories. From the overcoming of passions yearned for by Hellenism one moves through medieval landscapes inhabited by angels and demons, by psychic energies which, neglected, bring about full-blown psychosis or the equally terrifying normalization of the model citizen. Art and ethics are two creative outlets for these vital, impersonal forces, and the task of therapeutic work is their integration. A repudiation of the daimonic is on the other hand equivalent to narcissism, to wanting to believe that we are always delightful and upright, a stance which makes us project the daimonic outside ourselves.

The poet is of the devil's party, William Blake reminds us. The poet is also an accomplice of ethics, for the latter attacks being at its very roots. Genet wants to absorb the real within the imaginary and drown it, Sartre suggests, and the Sartrean scholar Borrello intimates that Genet becomes a poet in order to be as evil as possible. He uses poetry as the best possible means of destroying being.

Yet in destroying being the poet is free of the tyranny of ontology, which constitutes the chief obstacle to inaugurate ethics. This move is paradoxical because in drawing from the daimonic storehouse the poet finds the path to goodness beyond moralistic categories. The move is paradoxical for another reason: it attains impersonality via a profound engagement with subjectivity. Art activates reconciliation with the world, filtered through the androgynous mind of the artist.

How to describe a world without a self? Can one perceive the world objectively once the self is absent?

Poetry and Rebellion

Triviality is the reverse of poetry; it is the everyday colonized by the false needs and values of global capitalism and its veiled ideology.

Triviality is the reverse of aesthetics and ethics, rather than an ontic sub-product, a mucky splinter extracted from the shining hub of Being. We must be able to envision triviality outside the Heideggerian prison of authenticity/inauthenticity and reconfigure it as *colonization of the everyday*. The reports fed by the media are a faithful expression of triviality, i.e. a domain where crimes, accidents and natural catastrophes are discussed in a neutral tone, alongside gossip and 'culture'. The listener may continue to exist in the relative tranquillity of a sleep-walking condition, watching on screen the dehumanization of individuals via the proliferation of images and the banalization of disasters.

That triviality is the reverse of poetry does not mean that written poetry automatically escapes triviality, especially when a poem is ornament to a political or moral agenda. Poetry must be here understood as living presence, as disappearance of the subject (user, listener, and consumer) within the events of the world, as refusal of the cult of information and of the compulsory acquisition of data, of fragments of lived life acquired as goods – a process which in turn transforms the subject into an item to be purchased.

Poetry thus understood resists the objectification of humans and their sinister metamorphosis into news items. Poetic rupture reminds us of our immanent presence within phenomena and exposes us to the ineffable, to a poetic understanding of existence. As with early philosophy, such understanding is at once knowledge and love.

A poetic understanding of life is not accumulation of information or a way of *relating* to the world, because every relation is between subject and object. It invites us instead to identify with the world via a refusal of semantic modalities (denoting objects) and expressive modalities (communication of information). Poetic intuition frees us from the confinement of a world made falsely familiar; it opens up a perspective beyond mere psychological enrichment, a perspective which is understatedly close to aestheticism.

What makes poetic intuition ethical is a destructuring rigour which scales off the alleged solidity of the subject, who from being a *dandy* becomes an engaged subject – one that abandons identity and enters a process that Foucault calls *subjectification*. The engaged person and the aesthete share a sovereign love for the world, an aspiration to suspend the self alongside a recognition of flux, of one's own

117

ephemeral immanence within phenomena, hence the courage to embrace a multiplicity of perspectives polytheism and even what conventional thought calls evil and which in this context is the aesthetic rejection of the *status quo*. Unlike the *dandy*, the engaged subject transforms love for the world into love for justice, an engagement rigorous to the point of *cruelty* in Artaud's sense, i.e. of transformation of *écrit* as well as of *Scriptures* from abstraction to a physicality spurred on by the desire to respond to the silent ethical demand: as sensitive to a rebellious vocation as one would be to a sublime symphony which outlives each new regime. We find expression of this in Genet's support of the Palestinian cause even when he sensed, already in the early nineteen eighties, the prodromes of a metamorphosis which would turn the libertarian-Marxist guerrilla of the *fedayeen* into the seeds of Islamic militancy.

Poetry and rebellion have always been happy bedfellows. The rebel does not become a revolutionary; this is not because she no longer dares to claim power and effective change within the institutions, but because rebellion is invariably betrayed. The crystallization of rebellion into revolution is parallel to that of poetic imagination into religious dogma. As in the neologisms forged by sailors (not yet poets or people of the mainland) in their journeys, who might extract new sounds and symbols from the vast ocean, so the poetry of rebellion glitters as sun on the water. The language of rebellion outlives the solidification of laws and rules dictated by each new government. The dream of justice keeps surfacing within the prose of history as a tribute to the poetry of becoming – from the Paris commune to the Seattle anti-globalization movement, from the Arab Spring to the *Occupy* movement and any future ferment opening a breach in the alleged solidity of history. Hazy moon on an autumn night: emergence of the event, recognition of the infinity and ineffable nature of all phenomena.

Rebellion is codified; its images sold in shopping malls; yet new events appear. Genet heard the *fedayeen* intone improvised songs at night, mutual calls from one hill to the next, invented on the spot. The spontaneous songs of rebellion are fragments of a symphony whose notes we know by heart, whose score is glimpsed in our dreams. We make out its notes as we hear them on the barricades, when falling in love, or when in meditation we awake to the possi-

118

bilities of the real. The notes of an *event* wake us up to new horizons where liberations become reality. The notes of the *non-event* are instead narcotic, reactive, and seductive: they do not spur us towards conscious awakening, to liberative political action, to the generosity of ethics. The non-event is a reactive pseudo-rebellion which might cause catastrophes and upheavals yet maintains intact all the privileges of the ruling classes.

As with any genuine cultural movement as yet unaware of itself, phenomenology opened the curtain onto the horizon to reveal the miraculous concomitance between the self observing the horizon and the dawn. It became clear, thanks to the poetry of perception clarified by Merleau-Ponty, that solipsism is but an optical defect, a form of romantic misanthropy. The clarity of this perception did not last long, however. Soon the perceptive opening which exchanged the subject for being-in-the-world becomes an epistemological fetish and loses its essential meaning. In other words, *knowledge* now becomes the means to exteriority and alterity – Kierkegaard's mistake. In deciding to interpret knowledge as love (Plato) or appropriation (Hegel), we betray the existential dimension. Twentieth century thought attempted two ways out of this impasse: Heidegger laid down on the bed of contemplative inertia, defending *Dasein* from Bolshevism and American primitivism and unrepentantly supporting Nazism. Sartre chose activism and conscientious engagement, what Oreste Borrello calls "*a priori* engagement", walking a path which ended up reinforcing Cartesian rationalism, the "duty to clarify through reason the existence of all passions, starting with the basic one of dread in the face of nothingness"[3]. In order to renew such ethical and political engagement, it is perhaps necessary to use the *formal* Cartesian structure – utilizing the separation of the subject without slipping into dualistic ontology. One might in this way affirm a positive humanism, an anthropology in which the existent victoriously attacks history.[4] Such enquiry, though inspired by Husserl, distances itself from *disinterestedness*, a stance typical of foundational philosophies. A dispassionate enquiry, based on the practice of *epoché* and corroborated by intuition would reveal no less than the essence of things: a seductive hypothesis which reminds one of hermetic as well as *haiku* poetry, and of the intuitions of Jung's analytic psychology, which sees psyche communicated through images.

I believe it is essential not to allow oneself to be seduced by the sirens who promise us immediate knowledge of essences, no matter how revealing images might be. To be *se-duced* is to be lead elsewhere, away from the ineffability of phenomena and their reticence to provide symbols and symmetries behind the curtain of becoming. Geometry of lived life is not lived life: the geometrization of existence, effectively carried out via the Husserlian description of essences, dissolves the anti-metaphysical nature of phenomenology itself. The enquiry carried out by Merleau-Ponty has offered us the invaluable notion of *ambiguity* which evades the normative intervention of any of God's shadows; Sartrean enquiry translated this stance into ethical and historical engagement, emphasizing the link that most phenomenologists, with the exception of Merleau-Ponty had blatantly missed: historicity.

In the Meantime

The *meantime* is an interstice within linear time; not a moment of transcendence but one where immanence comes to be recognized as such; not the emergence of the noumenon but the full display of a phenomenon; not discovery of being but recognition of becoming. A moment of awareness reveals the extraordinary nature of the ordinary. Nothing particularly memorable or extraordinary happens. As in Michelangelo Antonioni's *dead time* sequences, there is no script, no dialogue, and no twists in the plot. The humanness of characters emerges in its ordinariness; the splendour and melancholy of a landscape comes into view. We enter a dimension beyond Husserlian temporalization and Bergsonian *durée*. There are perhaps similarities with the eternal recurrence, as the instant is enough for Nietzsche to recognize a province outside linear *and* circular time. This is not a mystical dimension but expression of the ambivalence of time poetically expressed, where even the subject of Sartrean paternity, the one able to *say* rather than *being said*, vanishes and is revealed as lexical fiction. The *I* is called into question in the accusative, Levinas would say, rather than in the conventional nominative form. An *I* does emerge, but solely in response to the event. And the event calls me into question when I come to understand the importance of my response to otherness.

Trans-descent

Engaged art and literature follow such an itinerary, entering time's interstices and acknowledging their ineffable nature. Some great works did of course follow the route of detachment and eternalism. There are two ways of going beyond: *transcendence* and *descent*. With the first, we risk recycling the ancient practice of life denigration in the name of the religious or spiritual ideal. With the second, we risk remaining stuck in the mires of delusion. Transcendence turns us into saints; descent turns us into sinners. But only sinners are given the chance of innocence regained which carries the charm of a lived life, whereas it is impossible to descend from a hallowed plinth.

An art reflecting the path of descent differs from transcendental art because it expresses the ambiguity of the real, its basic unknowability. It is no longer dominated by cognitive faculties and the acquisitive demands of light and knowledge but accompanies our descent into the night and the shadows. The duration and continuity of time is contradicted by the descent of the artist, the lover, and the meditator into the instant, where time metaphorically stands still. For this reason art, love and meditation imitate death, an event in which the future unfolds without the promise of actualization. Such an event is the *meantime*; the subject traverses it, while his shadow remains there forever.

We learn from Merleau-Ponty that pure receptivity and pure experience are fictions. The body is a *feeling felt*, at once subject and object. There is no need for willful expression, catharsis or emotional discharge. The body as it is is already poetry. To perceive is to incorporate and to express. Through our gestures we join a kinetic symphony – acting and at the same time being seen. No longer conceivable outside becoming, meaning is part of phenomena. The threshold leading us to meaning is integral to it.

In Praise of Desire

Ethics is not antithetic to desire but intimately linked to it. But what is desire? Mistrusted by religions and spiritual schools, desire is the antithesis of need. Whereas need transforms the other into the self-

121

same through labour, desire engenders the inscrutability of the future and emphasizes the distance separating me from the other, opening me up to longing. Desire is also different from pleasure. In pleasure we find the self-sufficency of a self equal to itself, the self-contentment which follows the illusory incorporation of otherness or, via an involutional process, the implosion which manufactures a self from nothingness. From the viewpoint of the subject, such creation is illusory. Yet in thinking of a human being I must consider her autonomous existence, her substantiality as existent *at the expense of* being.

Such consideration is non-rational; it is also plural. It differs from rationality *qua* plural, devoid of objectivity and neutrality. In the encounter with a self I fully recognize her individual, autonomous affirmation of life in her singular sphere. I see the tree and forget the forest. I disregard a neutral exaltation of life, race and nationality. Through my ethical rebellion I negate the tyranny of biology and the primacy of impersonality and affirm instead their opposite, my enticement towards encounter. Only in this way I may be able to move towards authentic atheism, i.e. towards a negation of totality. Only thus I lean over, exposed to otherness.

As with sexuality, the union expresses what was latent on the first encounter. Through such an encounter the originary function of philosophy is realized – encounter with the unknown across the jungle of fear, with the desire not giving in to need but transformed into longing.

Fear, desire, angst and ecstasy all force us towards such an encounter with the unknown, and it is here that we have a premonition of the other; it is here that identity vacillates in a relation of singular dignity, where the gap of distance is maintained, cultivated even, rather than filled. I am not speaking of mystical or ecstatic union, of scientific knowledge or even of inter-subjectivity. Encounter with alterity belongs to the poetic domain. It is born out of a philosophy of separation which utilizes the formal categories of Descartes and dares to think *infinity*. The name of a thought that can think infinity is desire. Not need, which is expectancy of satisfaction; not love, which wants union. It is the desiring of what the subject does not need, i.e. poetry, or *the realized love of desire which has remained desire*.

Desire affirms separation or transcendence, if by the latter we mean awareness of limitations – a transcendence *marked* and not filled by language. Such communication is not dialogue, where one addresses another as if she/he were another *I*, but instead poetic communication, *incident*. This is a communication which ignores being (hence totality) and fumbles for the inaccessible in the presence of the other, for Eurydice's face. Orpheus stops speaking, he stops singing; he turns, and in looking for otherness finds himself in the presence of death. Cain tries instead to solve the dilemma of alterity by killing Abel, but is still unable to reach him.

Encounter cannot take place by means of techniques but, on the contrary, it is only when techniques fail that the incident of poetic encounter with alterity becomes possible, and only in encountering alterity what we call *the present* may occur: the living moment rather than the decree of an end closing the past and opening the future. And yet we cannot inhabit the space of pure encounter with alterity: the lyric intensity is unsustainable beyond a few fortunate moments. But without it, as Buber reminds us, our existence is not living but surviving.

Not finding Anything is a Great Finding

Affirming the contingent nature of existence and describing experience with a new language are tasks fit for a poet. Gautama Siddhartha was one such poet, for he opened up a new path from the tangled branches of ancient Hindu beliefs.

Another was Nagarjuna, the thirteenth ancestor within the Zen tradition, who found ways to describe with a new language the correlation between the individual and the contingent reality of phenomena. Both the Buddha and Nagarjuna are poets because they opened up a new world by creating a new language. The Buddha, using at first familiar notions belonging to the cosmology and the psychology of his time, gradually introduced entirely new notions – above all *śūnyatā* (relativity or, more commonly, emptiness), a revolutionary assertion if we consider his epoch's insistence on both *ātman* (the alleged substantiality of the self raised to cosmic levels) and *eternalism*. As often happens, the idea of *śūnyatā* soon became a new

123

orthodoxy. It was then necessary for another poet to come along and re-describe the teachings of the Buddha in new terms, re-affirming *śūnyatā* in a non-doctrinaire fashion and in all its radical import. This person was Nagarjuna, who wrote:

> The Buddhas say that emptiness is abandoning opinions.
> Those who believe in emptiness are incurable.

One finds in Nagarjuna freedom from things but also freedom from nothingness or non-being, a freedom which gives birth to unconditional love. One becomes, as Shantideva reminds us, like a blind person who found a diamond on a pile of junk. Shantideva gave an ethical as well as affective turn to the implications present in the notion of *śūnyatā*: the latter not only invalidates (or at least loosens) the grip exerted on us by selfishness, but also generates empathy, so that an *empty* self becomes a *relating* self. Loving the world is the result of becoming no one.

Another poet within the Dharma tradition was Tsong Khapa, who examined the specificity of emptiness and highlighted that the emptiness of *śūnyatā* is absence of intrinsic existence: not a threshold to a mystical or transcendental dimension nor 'nothingness', but instead a more accurate perception of becoming. We do not find a thing but a process, and not finding anything is a great finding. Not finding anything substantial, consistent, anything that is not provisional and contingent is an extraordinary finding; consciousness itself is contingent: for Nagarjuna, it emerges from the eyes and the multicoloured forms as a child from his parents.

Phenomenology of Abjection

There are different kinds of conversion. The western tradition has used Cartesian doubt, valuable in extricating oneself from superstition, but ultimately a doubt that does not doubt itself encourages the superstition of hard science. The phenomenological tradition has used suspension, with its manifold directions, from hunting for the essence of things to ethical and political engagement. To doubt and suspension one could add abjection, a move (*ab-jacere*, to throw away, to reject) which for Sartre does not lead to the Cartesian cogito or Husserl's transcendental consciousness but to a high-voltage existence.

The Sartrean notion is not mere provocation but must be considered seriously in formulating a radical ethics. Without such a movement of lucid revolt, ethics would repeat the mistake of morality, that handmaid of transcendence and reason, and would evade the initiation of fire Genet calls for when he invites us to feel directly on our skin the suffering of the human condition.

To be an outcast, or an abject and immoral person does not automatically qualify one to being the agent of a meaningful and radical conversion. In order to do that a second move is necessary, an act of anti-metaphysical rebellion, of voluntary descent into phenomena and becoming: this is a poetic act, absurd and unmotivated, without which the rebellion of the oppressed flows into new alienated acquisition or the vulgar immoralism which forever joins the petty thief to the capitalist.

Revolt is related to evil, Plato's bastard dream, hypothetically understood as poetic exile from being and from having, as *betrayal* of the illusory values of being and having. Betrayal makes Genet's aestheticism undoubtedly *evil*, but it eventually turns it into humane engagement.

The deserter, universally despised, has access to a unique form of perception; he is a true rebel without a cause, a shipwrecked who fully understands the fragile certainties of life on the mainland, and who in his abjection discerns the fact that morality is an illusion.

Still Untimely

Ethical rebellion undermines metaphysics at its roots by affirming groundlessness; it questions epistemology and the fetish of knowledge by affirming not-knowing. This is not Socratic not-knowing, which is after all dialectical artifice, but the not-knowing of Zen, that is, affirmation of the unknowability of existence and of existents.

Such an opening belongs to the category Nietzsche calls *the untimely*: irruption of becoming within history, actualization of the future within the present, dissolution of noumena and affirmation of phenomena. The emergence of pure phenomena is an awakening: the awakening of the Buddha who recognizes the non-substantiality of every thing; the awakening of the subject who in the vulnerability of encounter with otherness ceases as a subject and becomes an individual; the awakening of a collectivity in the revolutionary *event*. The emergence of the phenomenon is the poetic emergence of the real. A true opening, the sky furrowed by lightning revealing the miserliness of bourgeois existence: sleep-walking, solipsistic and cradled to death by the useful.

The dissemination carried out by information technology and global networking must not deceive us. Technologically advanced, universally within reach, our dominant way of being is still primitive and territorial, confirming rather than disproving Descartes' error.

Our way of being is still solipsistic, and for this reason the difference between solipsism and individuality must be better understood. Montaigne's self-examination does without the objectivity of the narrator who writes in the third person. It is a form of observation which gives birth to the individuality of self-discovery, with an emphasis on the uniqueness of the individual and the non-substantial nature of identity. Descartes' method, though individual and subjective, is founded instead on the impersonality and alleged universality of reason. Montaigne underlines originality, goes in search of the unique voice which may describe the world anew, whereas Descartes imposes on the individual the impersonal order of science. Alongside a circumstantial study of the self, Montaigne champions deep friendship. Writing and solitary meditation are pale reflections of the dialogue between friends, which constitutes the origin of philosophy itself.

The study of self proposed by Dōgen similarly leads one to letting go of the self; not to neglecting the self, because *studium* is love, and to study the self must also mean to love the self. Abandoning the self in the name of spiritual practice, before having studied it, is a form of neglect, which forgets the transient nature of phenomena and deserts individuality, thus abandoning the domain of freedom and responsibility. Both pollute the innocence of becoming with the poisoned chalices of scientism and religious dogma. The refusal to abandon individuality belongs to the poetic domain. It restores us to

126

living reality and shatters the prosaic abstractions of both religion and science.

Epilogue

There is a thread linking together the self, the other, and the world. It is more than a thread, in fact: they are essentially one. To simply say that they are one, however, is too vague a proposition, for each of these is particular and offers particular revelations. I have tried to explore these three dimensions throughout the book, at times in a deliberately non-linear fashion given that their boundaries are often blurred.

In **Part I** we have seen how a closer look at the self reveals its fluidity, its multiplicity. Instead of an essence, we find a series of events. When the self truly encounters the other, however, it paradoxically comes into being as a seemingly separate entity. This separation is not the alleged solidity of individualism but represents instead the gap separating the self from the other; it is a space of anxiety and vertigo – the risk of desire, the call of responsibility.

With the first introspective move we deconstruct the self – we study the self and in doing so recognize its peculiarities. This study is curiosity *and* love, inquiry and compassion. Interiority is approached with a sense of awe and irony, with a desire to become intimate with it. The main inspirations here are Montaigne and the Buddha. To approach the inner life with an attitude of inquiry is different from the more conventional approach of repentance. The latter has been the dominant mode of established religions and has influenced philosophy, psychology, science and culture even when these use a secular language. The difference between inquiry and repentance is subtle yet significant. It is the difference between learning and denigration, between accepting and chastising. Granted, both attitudes can be transformative, but the former does not set an ideal against which one's imperfections are measured, nor does it wait for things to 'go wrong' before embarking on a path of meditation and study.

128

In **Part II** we have seen how the previous stance brims over into the socio-political sphere: when, through study and meditation, the self is accepted and understood – including its less positive, more troublesome aspects – the probability of projecting one's disowned characteristics onto others is less. When, through genuine encounter, it becomes clear that the presence of the other is essential to the birth of the self, the other is not ostracized but welcomed. As we have seen, the self becomes the self through welcoming the other. It abandons individualism and *ipseity* (self-bound identity) for individuality. It abandons the defensiveness and aggression of the former in favour of a more inclusive and adaptive sense of self which takes into account its fluid and paradoxical nature as well as the truth of interdependence.

Similarly by welcoming the non-citizen (i.e. the migrant, the stranger, the foreigner etc.), the bourgeois – a self bound by its social status and possessions – becomes a *citizen* in Hannah Arendt's sense, released from the irrelevant constraints of ethnic, religious and racial identity. This is a radical ethical stance of *xenophilia*, or love of strangers (the opposite of xenophobia), which can be translated into pragmatic social engagement, for instance by questioning the legitimacy of borders which impede the free movement of people across nation-states.

In **Part III** we have seen how ethics must be linked to aesthetics and the symbolic domain. The reason for this is partly in order to circumvent the now predictable turn of most notions of freedom into new modes of oppression. The symbolic domain also prevents us to take a too literal assumption of responsibility which would become co-opted by the universal guilt of established religions. Response to otherness is of course political. But it is first of all *poetic*. The poet evoked in **Part III** is Hölderlin, who invites us to 'dwell poetically on this earth'.

If we can remember our essential condition as *guests* on this earth we stand a chance of becoming good *hosts* and true citizens.

NOTES

Introduction

1 Goldstein, 1995.
2 Schwartz, 1997.
3 Nussbaum, 1994.

PART I A PLACE IN THE SUN

 1 Tedeschi, 2000.
 2 Pasolini, 1968, p. 83.
 3 Here I borrow, and partly adapt, Maurice Blanchot's notion on the topic. See Blanchot, 1993.
 4 Bauman, 1993.
 5 Stern, 1995.
 6 Gadamer, 2012.
 7 Jankélévitch, 2005.
 8 Pasolini, 1972.
 9 Batchelor, 2007, p. 8.
10 Nishida Kitaro 1992.
11 Nietzsche, 1996, *II*, 17, p. 67.
12 Bazzano, 2009, pp. 145–53.
13 Critchley, 2007, p. 78.
14 Plessner is one of the exponents, with Max Scheler, Arnold Gehlen and Kurt Stavenhagen, of "philosophical anthropology" (see Schnädelbach, 1984).
15 Plessner, 1970, pp. 36–40.

PART II A HUMAN REVOLUTION

 1 Phillips, 2012, p. 14.
 2 Critchley, 2007, p. 61.
 3 Private logic is Adler's term, opposed to common sense. Cf. Ansbacher and Ansbacher, 1964.

4 Batchelor, 1997.
5 Schwartz, 1997.
6 Schwartz, 1997, p. 54.
7 Bazzano, 2006.
8 Schwartz, 1997, p. 71.
9 Schneider, 1984.
10 Rose 2005, p. 74.
11 Anderson, 2006, p. 37.
12 Gellner, 1965.
13 Anderson, 2006, p. 143.
14 Schwartz, 1997.
15 Schwartz, 1997, p 124.
16 Cf. T.R. Flynn, 2005.
17 Rose, 2005.
18 Buber, 1983.
19 Arendt, 1978, p. 92.
20 Derrida, 1994.
21 Nairn, 1977, pp. 155–56.
22 Anderson, 2006, p.160.
23 Michelet, 1982, p. 268.
24 Anderson , 2006, p. 204.
25 Critchley, 2007, p. 13.
26 Critchley, 2007.
27 Cf. De Beauvoir, 1976.
28 Jeremy Harding, "Europe at Bay", *London Review of Books* 34 (3), 9 February 2012, pp. 3–11.

PART III LIVING POETICALLY ON THIS EARTH

1 Voll Verdienst, doch dictherish, / wohnet der Mensch /auf dieser Erde. Full of merit, yet poetically/ man dwells on this Earth. Some translate 'Voll Verdienst' with 'Though he has to earn a living' rather than 'Full of merit'. Quoted in *Mythos and Logos*,
http ://mythosandlogos.com/.html. Retrieved 12 March 2012.
2 Cf. Heidegger, 1971, pp. 213–29, and Wallace Stevens in Kermode, 2003, pp. 143–159.
3 Borrello, 1962, p. 158, my translation.
4 Borrello, 1962, p. 158.

BIBLIOGRAPHY

Masao Abe, *Zen and the Modern World*, Honolulu: University of Hawai Press, 2003.

Giorgio Agamben, *Homo Sacer: Sovereign Power and Bare Life*, Stanford, CA: Stanford University Press, 1998.

Benedict Anderson , *Imagined Communities: Reflections on the Origin and Spread of Nationalism*, London: Verso, 2006.

H. L. Ansbacher, & R. Ansbacher, *The Individual Psychology of Alfred Adler*, New York: Harper & Row, 1964.

Hannah Arendt, *The Jew as Pariah: Jewish Identity and Politics in the Modern Age,* New York: Grove Press, 197

———, *Eichmann in Jerusalem:a Report on the Banality of Evil*, London: Penguin, 1993.

Gaston Bachelard, *The Poetics of Space*, Boston, MA: Beacon Press, 1994.

Alain Badiou, *Ethics: An Essay on the Understanding of Evil,* London: Verso, 2001.

Etienne Balibar and Immanuel Wallerstein, *Race, Nation, Class: Ambiguous Identities*, London: Verso, 1991.

Stephen Batchelor, *Buddhism without Beliefs*, New York: Riverhead, 1997.

——— *Verses from the Centre: A Buddhist Vision of the Sublime,* New York: Riverhead, 2000.

——— *Living with the Devil,* New York: Riverhead, 2007.

Zygmunt Bauman, *Post-modern Ethics*, Cambridge, MA: Basil Blackwell, 1993.

Manu Bazzano, *Buddha is dead: Nietzsche and the Dawn of European Zen,* Brighton, Portland: Sussex Academic Press, 2006.

——— "Brave New Worlding: A response to Practicing Existential Psychotherapy: The Relational World by Ernesto Spinelli", *Journal of Existential Analysis*, 20 (1), London: SEA, 2009.

Walter Benjamin, *One Way Street*, London:Penguin, 2008.

Ludwig Binswanger, *Being in the World: Selected Papers*, New York: Harper & Row, 1968.

Maurice Blanchot, *The Infinite Conversation*, Minneapolis and London: University of Minnesota Press, 1993.

Oreste Borrello, *La Psicanalisi esistenziale e il problema dell'arte in J. P. Sartre: Aspetti dell'estetica odierna*, Naples: 1962.

Martin Buber, *A Land of Two peoples: Martin Buber on Jews and Arabs*, New York: Oxford University Press, 1983.

———— *I and Thou*, London: Continuum, 2008.

Judith Butler, *Precarious Life*, London, New York: Verso, 2004.

Simon Critchley, *Infinitely Demanding,* London: Verso, 2007.

Guy Debord, *The Society of the Spectacle*, London: Rebel Press, 1969.

Alessandro Dal Lago, *Non-Persons: the Exclusion of Migrants in a Global Society*, Milan: Ipoc, 2009.

Simone de Beauvoir, *The Ethics of Ambiguity*, New York: Kensington Publishing, 1976.

Angelo Del Boca, *Italiani, brava gente?*, Milano: Neri Pozza, 2005.

Gilles Deleuze, *Pourparlers*, Paris: Les Editions de Minuit, 1990.

Jacques Derrida, *Specters of Marx*, New York: Routledge, 1994.

———— *Adieu to Emmanuel Levinas*, Stanford, CA: Stanford University Press, 1997.

Terry Eagleton, *After Theory*, New York: Basic Books, 2003.

T.R. Flynn, *Sartre, Foucault and Historical Reason: A Poststructuralist Mapping of History*, Chicago: The University of Chicago Press, 2005.

Michel Foucault, *Discipline and Punish: The Birth of the Prison*, London: Vintage, 1973.

———— *Le gouvernement de soi et des autres, Cours au College de France, 1982–1983*, Paris: Gallimard/Seuil, 2008.

———— *Le courage de la vérité: Le government de soi et des autres II, Cours au College de France, 1983–1984*, Paris: Gallimard/Seuil, 2009.

Jean Genet, *Captif amoureux*, Paris: Gallimard, 1986.

Hans-Georg Gadamer, *Truth and Method*, London: Continuum, 2012.

Ernest Gellner, *Thought and Change,* London: Weidenfeld & Nicolson, 1965.

Bernie Glassman, *Bearing Witness: A Zen Master's Lessons in Making Peace,* New York: Bell Tower, 1998.

Kurt Goldstein, *The Organism*, New York: Zone Books, 1995.

Jeremy Harding, "Europe at Bay", *London Review of Books* 34 (3) 9 February 2012, pp. 3–11.

Michael Hardt, "Militant Life", *New Left Review 64,* July–August 2010, pp 151–160, London: Verso, 2010.

N. Harris, *Thinking the Unthinkable: The Immigration Myth Exposed*, London: I.B. Tauris, 2002.

Martin Heidegger, *Poetry, Language, Thought*, New York: Harper & Row, 1971.

———— *Being and Time*, Malden, MA: Blackwell, 1962.

F. Holderlin, "Though he has to earn a living . . ." retrieved 13 March 2012, http://mythosandlogos.com/Holderlin.html.

S. P. Huntington, *The Clash of Civilizations: Remaking of World Order*, New York: Simon & Schuster, 1996.

Edmund Husserl, *Cartesian Meditations: An Introduction to Phenomenology*, Dordrecht: Kluwer Academic Publishers, 1993.

Geoffry Hill, *Scenes from Comus,* London: Penguin, 2005.

Vladimir Jankélévitch, *Forgiveness*, Chicago: University of Chicago Press, 2005.

————*Music and the Ineffable*, Princeton, NJ: Princeton University Press, 2003.

Frank Kermode, *Pieces of my Mind*, London: Allen Lane, 2003.

Ernesto Laclau & Chantal Mouffe, *Hegemony and Socialist Strategy: Towards a Radical Democratic Politics*, London: Verso, 1985.

Emmanuel Levinas, *On Escape*, Stanford, CA: Stanford University Press, 2003.

———— *Totality and Infinity: an Essay on Exteriority*, Pittsburgh: Duquesne University, Press, 1961.

———— *Alterity and Transcendence*, New York: Columbia University Press, 1999.

Bernard Lewis, "The Roots of Muslim Rage," *The Atlantic* 266 (3), September 1990, pp. 47–60.

Knud Løgstrup, *The Ethical Demand*, Notre Dame, Indiana: University of Notre Dame Press, 1997.

David MacMahon, *The Making of Buddhist Modernism*, New York: Oxford University Press, 2008.

Philip Marfleet, *Refugees in a Global Era*, New York: Palgrave Macmillan, 2006.

Eric Matthews, *The Philosophy of Merleau-Ponty*, Chesham, Bucks: Acumen, 2002.

Karl Marx and Friedrich Engels, *Marx-Engels Werke Band I*, Berlin: Dietz, 1988.

Karl Marx and Friedrich Engels, *Manifesto of the Communist Party*, Retrieved 16 March 2012, http://www.anu.edu.au/polsci/marx/classics/manifesto.html.

Karl Marx, *Early Political Writings*, Cambridge, MA: Cambridge University Press, 1994.

Rollo May, *Love and Will*, New York: W.W. Norton & Company, 1969.

Jules Michelet, *Ouvres Completes*, Vol. XXI, Paris: Flammarion, 1982.

Tom Nairn, *The Break-up of Britain,* London: New Left Books, 1977.

Friedrich Nietzsche, *On the Genealogy of Morals*, New York: Oxford University Press, 1996.

Kitaro Nishida, *An Inquiry into the Good*, New Haven, CT: Yale University Press, 1992.

Martha Nussbaum, "Patriotism and Cosmopolitanism", *Boston Review* Retrieved 11 January 2012, http://bostonreview. net/BR19.5/ nussbaum.php; http://faculty.cape-bretonu.ca/philosophy/301/pdfs/1%20 Patriotism. pdf, 1994.

Pier Paolo Pasolini, *Empirismo eretico*, Milano: Garzanti, 1972.

———— *Teorema*, Milano: Garzanti, 1968.

Adam Phillips, "Judas' Gift: in Praise of Betrayal", *London Review of Books*, Vol. 34, No. 1, 5 January 2012.

Plato, *Republic*, New York: Oxford University Press, 1993.

Helmuth Plessner, *Laughing and Crying: A Study of the Limits of Human Behavior*, Evanston, IL: Northwestern University Press, 1970.

Jacques Rancière, "The Aesthetic Revolution and its Outcomes", *New Left Review*, no. 14, March–April 2002, London: Verso, 2002.

Antonella Randazzo, *Roma Predona: il colonialismo italiano in Africa, 1870–1943*, Milano: Kaos Edizioni, 2006.

John Rawls, *Lectures on the History of Moral Philosophy*, Cambridge, MA: Harvard University Press, 2000.

Ernest Renan, *Oeuvres Completes*, Paris: Calmann-Levy, 1947.

Jacqueline Rose, *The Question of Zion*, Princeton, NJ: Princeton University Press, 2005.

Edward Said, *Power, Politics, and Culture*, London: Bloomsbury, 2004.

———— "The Clash of Ignorance" *The Nation* 22 October 2001.

———— "Confini incerti", *Corriere della Sera*, 30 September 2001.

Friedrich Schiller, *On the Aesthetic Education of Man*, New York: Dover Publications, 2004.

David Simpson, "Ruin and Redemption", *London Review of Books*, Vol. 27, No. 12, 23 June 2005.

Herbert Schnädelbach, *Philosophy in Germany 1831–1933*, Cambridge, MA: Cambridge University Press, 1984.

David Schneider, *A Critique of the Study of Kinship*, University of Michigan

Press, Ann Arbor, MI, 1984.

E.M. Schur, *Crimes without Victims*, Englewood Cliffs, NJ: Prentice Hall, 1965.

Regina Schwartz, *The Curse of Cain: The Violent Legacy of Monotheism*, Chicago: University of Chicago Press, 1997.

Lev Shestov, *All Things are Possible*, London: Martin Secker, 1920.

Daniel Stern, *The Interpersonal World of the Infant: A View from Psychoanalysis and Developmental Psychology*, New York: Basic Books, 1995.

Joseph Stigliz, *Globalization and its Discontents* London: Penguin, 2002.

Gianfranco Tedeschi, *L'ebraismo e la psicologia analitica: Rivelazione teologica e Rivelazione psicologica*, Firenze: Giuntina, 2000.

Max Weber, *The Vocation Lectures*, Indianapolis, Indiana: Hackett Publishing Company, 2004.

ABOUT THE AUTHOR

Manu Bazzano received a B.A. in Philosophy in 1980. He is a qualified person-centred/existential psychotherapist, counsellor and supervisor (MBACP, UKCP) in private practice in North London, and a Zen Buddhist monk in both the Soto and Rinzai traditions.

A lecturer in humanistic psychotherapy and modern European philosophy, he regularly contributes to magazines such as *Therapy Today*, *PCEP*, *Dharma,* and *Journal of Existential Analysis*. He edited the best-selling anthologies *Zen Poems* (2002) and *Haiku for Lovers (*2004*)* and published several books, including: *Buddha is Dead: Nietzsche and the Dawn of European Zen* (2006) and the novella *The Speed of Angels* (2009). Website: www.manubazzano.com

INDEX

Eliot, George, 16
elites, 6
Ellul, Jacques, 22
embarrassment, 12
embodiment, 24, 40, 56
empathy, 16, 40
empiricism, 43
emptiness, 51, 123–4
encounter
  celebration of, 107
  with otherness, 6, 23, 30–2, 36,
    40–1, 43, 56, 61–2, 64, 71, 75,
    82, 122–3, 128, 129
  separation as key factor, 21, 122,
    128
  and techniques, 64, 123
  vulnerability of, 28, 61, 126
endogamy, 81–2
enjoy mantra, 54
Enlightenment
  emergence of nationalism, 84
  reason, 43
  utopian principles, 30
enlightenment, emphasis on, 1
entelechy, 50
Epictetus, 115
Epicurus, 9, 49
epidemics, 103
epimeleia heautou, 113
epistemology, 25, 51, 125
epoché, 26, 40, 57, 119
equality, 62, 74
equanimity, 95
Erfarhung, 48, 90
Erlebnis, 90
Eros, 15, 23, 40, 55, 56–7, 64, 107
erotic passion, 55
Esau, 78, 82
essence
  of ethics, 19
  human nature, 76
  Husserl, 105, 120
  intuition of, 40
  quest for, 28
estrangement, 33, 46

eternalism, 44, 72, 121, 123
eternity, 13, 37, 44
ethical action, 39, 75
ethical commitment, 31, 90
ethical demand, 30, 51, 52–5, 63,
  110, 118
ethical imperative, 34
ethical subjectivity, 90
ethics
  active, 50
  and aesthetics, 7, 105–7, 110–11,
    113, 129
  appreciation of the everyday,
    19–20
  as art, 39, 43, 72, 110–11, 116
  autonomous, 49–50
  birth of, 48
  bourgeois, 42
  defined, 2
  and desire, 121
  different phases of, 27
  encounter with otherness, 2, 3,
    43
  exteriority as reality, 2
  good and evil, 18, 33
  hedonic, 49
  Hellenism, 34
  heteronomous, 48–9
  human domain, 51–2
  impermanence, 36
  lack of essence, 19
  Levinas, 2–3
  and metaphysics, 73
  misunderstanding of, 34
  and phenomenology, 26, 105
  philosophy's dissolution into, 43
  as poetry, 107, 116
  and politics, 89–90, 92, 95–6
  primacy over ontology, 19, 95
  and psychology, 28
  rational, 49
  rebirth of, 17–18
  religious dictates, 18
  and rules, 54
  and time, 37, 106

Mnemosyne, 107
modernism, 23, 25
modernity, 89
money, 61, 73, 74, 75
monogamy, 78, 80
monolatry, 6, 18, 78, 79
    see also deity; God
monotheism, 6, 9, 77, 78, 80, 81
    see also deity; God
Montaigne, Michel de, 4, 126, 128
moral philosophy, 29
moral relativism, 15, 29
moralism, 114
morality
    attribute of the interval, 34
    bourgeois, 2, 12, 63
    conscience, 2
    defined, 2
    derived from external authority, 48
    dismantling of, 2
    ethical sphere outside, 89
    good and evil, 116
    high demands of, 30
    interiority-as-repentance, 2
    Kantianism, 29, 30
    post-metaphysical era, 29
    re-personalization of, 30
    versus ethics, 2
moralizing projection, 23
Moses, 80
multi-culturalism, 100, 103
multinational corporations, 54
multiplicity
    Biblical interpretation, 78
    embodiment, 56
    humanistic psychology, 19
    of the psyche, 40
    and the self, 11, 55, 128
    vision of time, 85
Mumonkan, 33
Muses, 2, 107
museums of living, 64
music, 43, 110–11
mysticism, 20
myths

of belonging, 17
    biblical, 83
    hostility towards otherness, 6
    of monotheism, 77
    poetry/poets, 108
    of the soil, 79

Nagarjuna, 123, 124
narcissism, 116
narrow-mindedness, 97–8
nation-states
    control of people's movement, 100,
        102–3
    hospitality, 58
    human rights, 96
    and identity, 77, 83–7
    insubstantiality of, 4
    and memory, 87, 88–9
nationalism
    delusion of self-sufficiency, 86
    generations of, 88
    historical destiny, 88
    origins of, 6, 84
    rhetoric, 85
nationalist dogma, 12
natural sciences, 22, 27–8
Nazism, 14, 97, 98, 119
necessity, 43–5, 46, 49, 53, 109
need, 12, 40, 121–2
negative capability, 106
neo-Darwinians, 51
neuro-scientism, 22
neutrality, 26, 30, 122
new age congregations, 16
new age mysticism, 21
New Age obscurantism, 112
new age spirituality, 72, 92
Nietzsche, Friedrich Wilhelm
    Buddha is dead, 3
    bad conscience, 62, 90
    death of God, 95
    deconstruction of morals, 2
    embodied psychology, 27
    ethics and aesthetics, 113
    faith, 45